ALCOHOL RECOVERY FOR WOMEN

7 ESSENTIAL STEPS TO QUIT DRINKING, FIND THE ROAD TO RECOVERY, AND TAKE CONTROL OF YOUR NEW SOBER LIFE

RUBI PAGE

CONTENTS

Introduction   7

1. EXAMINING THE PROBLEM   15
   Why Do We Drink?   15
   Main Reasons for Alcohol Abuse   38

2. STEP 1: TRY TO UNDERSTAND
   YOURSELF   51
   Understanding Where You Are in
   Addiction   51
   Self-Assessment Tool   70

3. STEP 2: CREATE A PLAN   79
   Develop a Plan to Help You Quit
   Drinking   79
   Creating SMART Goals   81

4. STEP 3: PLAN AND PREPARE FOR
   DETOX   95
   Preparing Your Mind and Body for Detox   95
   When Should You Consider Rehab?   106

5. STEP 4: MANAGING SOCIAL EVENTS   117
   Overcoming Shame and Staying Sober at
   Social Events   117

6. STEP 5: RECOGNIZE THE HIGHS AND
   THE LOWS   127
   Understanding Your Good Days and Your
   Bad Days   127

7. STEP 6: USE DISTRACTIONS TO YOUR
   ADVANTAGE   143
   How to Use Distractions to Help You
   Fight Cravings   143

8. STEP 7: CREATE A VALUABLE
   NETWORK   157
   Leaning On Your Friends and Family and
   Being a Part of Support Groups   157

   Conclusion   171
   References   177

A FREE GIFT FOR YOU!

9 Common Mistakes To Avoid In Early Alcohol Recovery

Just scan the QR code below to claim Your free gift!

INTRODUCTION

Sometimes, when you're in a dark place, you think
you've been buried, but you've actually been planted.

— CHRISTINE CAINE

Alcoholism is a worldwide dilemma that has taken over millions of people's lives and destroyed families. It isn't only a cause for concern among men, but also among women. Nearly 13% of women reported they binge-drink at least four times a month, consuming over 5 drinks per binge. Practically half of all adult women in the United States admit to drinking alcohol within the past 30 days. Delving deeper into the statistics, nearly

8% of women aged between 18 and 25 reported that they had a drinking disorder (*Excessive Alcohol Use and Risks to Women's Health | CDC*, 2020). In this modern age, alcohol has become increasingly popular among women, and it isn't hard to miss because it is now readily available. Going for a lunch date out with friends, attending a work Christmas party, or being invited to a barbecue at your family member's home. Alcohol will be present during these situations, just to mention a few.

After a long, exhausting day at work, you walk into your home looking forward to some peace. But at the back of your mind, you know that relaxation is far from your reality. Instead, your reality comprises kids fighting and shouting all day long, you rushing home from work to get supper ready on time, and dealing with a marriage that has been rocky lately because of the constant arguing. Single moms, with no help or support, find it extremely stressful to cope with the pressures of being the breadwinner in the family and the primary caregiver to their children. Also, women who have experienced trauma during their childhood, including their teenage years, experience pain that comes from a lot of unresolved issues buried deep inside themselves.

Domestic violence from partners in a relationship or marriage, or being emotionally abused and cheated on multiple times, can contribute significantly to alcohol abuse in women. Single women also fall into addiction because of the negative influence of friends. Maybe they are trying to fit in with the crowd at work, or maybe they have intense family issues. It doesn't matter if you are married or single, young or old; addiction can happen to anyone. This is, unfortunately, the reality for so many women today. The pressures of life just keep piling on, becoming heavier and heavier. Who wouldn't feel overwhelmed? Who wouldn't crack under pressure? It is normal to want to have a drink or two at the end of a stressful day. It takes the edge off, helping you wind down and feel more relaxed: being lost in that moment where there's no stress, no frustration, or anger, and it becomes the only thing you look forward to in your day. And as relaxing as alcohol can be, it becomes addictive for some women. A fatal attraction begins, and women find themselves drawn towards alcohol because of the level of comfort and confidence it provides. You don't even see it, but quickly, a relationship with alcohol develops. It all starts off great, but we all know that it isn't going to end well. It's a relationship that you never thought you would have found yourself in. Eventually, alcohol becomes a crutch that you cannot do without. The fine line between drinking for enjoyment and drinking just to feel normal becomes blurry fast, and addiction sets in.

There are around 15 million adults in the US who have developed problems with drinking. Alcohol addiction is on the rise worldwide; however, it is especially prevalent in America. People have always used alcohol to celebrate something significant in their lives, such as a birthday, wedding, or landing a dream job. However, nowadays, people use alcohol to help them get through difficult phases in their lives, such as experiencing divorce and dealing with the death of a loved one. When used in these circumstances, alcohol can become instantly addictive. I can understand how difficult it is to heal from emotional pain that completely takes over your life. It gets even worse if you don't have the support of friends and family around you. Spiraling into addiction is easy, and most women don't even realize that they have a problem until it affects their lives in a big way. Such was the case with Sandy, who suffered with her alcohol addiction for years.

Sandy was an alcoholic who believed that she was her best self when she was under the influence of alcohol. Her shyness and poor self-confidence no longer existed whenever she drank, and she felt happy and free. Sober, she never spoke to strangers and she always held back from being her true, authentic self. But when she drank, she felt confident in herself. All this came from her regular use of alcohol. Sandy strongly believed that alcohol helped her cope with her fears, and she quickly developed an alcohol addiction.

Believe it or not, Sandy started drinking when she was very young. She could hardly remember her teenage days. It all was such a blur to her, and she became a heavy drinker during her college years. Sandy couldn't hold down a job for more than three months. She would often become bored and attend work under the influence of alcohol. Her relationships were also affected by her drinking. She couldn't be in a committed relationship because she always gave her drinking priority over anyone else. Boyfriends came and went; some relationships lasted longer than others only because these guys shared a passion for alcohol. Since she couldn't work, Sandy stayed at home and spent most of her time sleeping, drinking, and watching TV. She tried taking up a few short courses. However, the urge to drink again arose when the pressures of studying became too much to handle. She began drinking secretly and allowed her addiction to take over her life. She dropped out of her studies because she could no longer concentrate or keep to her deadlines. Her alcoholism took over her life and destroyed everything that meant so much to her.

Life became miserable for Sandy. She blamed everyone else for her addiction to alcohol. She blamed her mother, her studies, and her failed career, and she always thought that she would be better off if only she had a good job, or if she found the right person to spend her life with, or if she could pay back all the money she owed people. There were always those "if only" thoughts at the back of her mind. But she would never take a leap of faith to help herself overcome her addiction. Sandy always resisted getting help for her addiction. She was always in denial. Until one day, Sandy received a wake-up call that would change her life forever. She was supposed to fetch her sister's kids from school one rainy afternoon because her sister was working late, but Sandy drank so much that she blacked out and forgot about the children. The kids walked home in the rain and fell sick because of that; one of them ended up in hospital because he developed pneumonia.

Sandy felt extremely guilty, so she made a huge decision to start her journey to overcoming addiction. She called up The Salvation Army to see if she could get some help. She put aside all her excuses and finally took the hard steps to turn her life around. You can do this too, but the desire to change must come from the heart. Everyone has a different story to share about their struggle with addiction. You can make the change that is needed to turn your life around. I understand it isn't easy to take the first steps to overcome addiction. But once you see just how beneficial it would be for you, the process will be easier to embrace. Just after one month of not consuming alcohol, your body recovers. Your sleeping patterns will improve, your moods will stabilize, and you will feel more energetic and alive. Another significant benefit you will reap is saving the money you spend on alcohol.

I have been down that road of addiction, and I know how long the journey was for me. I am 20 years sober, and I am doing better than ever. I wanted to help other women who have also suffered because of their addiction. The steps that I will share with you in this book have proven to make a difference in my life. Now that you have taken the first step towards your recovery by reading this book, prepare yourself for a life free from alcohol addiction. Yes! It is possible. If I could fight my addiction, there is no reason you can't fight yours. I am here to support you and guide you on this journey. You are not alone, and you can accomplish your goals by staying committed to this process.

Even celebrities such as Naomi Campbell and Bella Hadid gave up drinking alcohol and have shared their life-changing experiences. Bella Hadid suffers from crippling anxiety and mental health issues, and she used to drink alcohol to help her socialize with people. But since she stopped drinking, she feels so much more in control of her life and clearer about her decisions. Naomi Campbell had a critical phase in her addiction to alcohol. She found it hard to cope with the pressures of the fashion industry, and she used alcohol to help her stay calm. But things spiraled out of control, and she joined AA and gave up on alcohol. Life has changed tremendously for her since she took those steps, and she feels so happy that she made the right decision earlier on in her life (Savin, 2020). These steps that I will share with you will change your life forever! It's never too late to make the right decision for yourself. Get ready for your new life. Change is coming sooner than expected.

1

EXAMINING THE PROBLEM

WHY DO WE DRINK?

I guess there is no right answer to this question. People don't just wake up one day and decide to become alcoholics. Only you understand why you started drinking. The internal struggle with your emotions, with your memories, and with your health has contributed to your addiction in some way or another. Alcohol abuse is more common than you think. Nearly 17% of men and 8% of women will become addicted to alcohol in their life. So, trying to find a universal reason people become addicted to alcohol would not be possible. The reason would be more personal rather than universal.

It is crucial that you understand why you drink. If you cannot pinpoint a reason, then you won't be able to free yourself and take control of your life. To overcome the problem, identify it first. We create every solution by keeping the problem in mind, because the solution has to target the root of the problem and fix it for good. You have to face yourself and dig deep into your heart. Get down to the source of the problem, and don't be ashamed to admit where you went wrong. This chapter will help you through this process. All you have to do is be true to yourself and trust the process.

What Is Alcoholism?

Alcoholism, also known as alcohol use disorder, is the most severe form of alcohol use. There are different levels of alcoholism, ranging from mild to severe. When a person has an alcohol use disorder, they cannot manage their alcohol intake, and they will feel as if they cannot make it through the day without the aid of alcohol. If you feel withdrawal symptoms after a long period of no drinking, that would be a sign that you are addicted to alcohol. Most people aren't ready to accept that their alcohol consumption causes problems in their personal and professional lives. Every time they drink, they have to consume more to get the same effect as last time. If your alcohol intake puts your health and safety at risk, then it is alcoholism.

What Does Unhealthy Alcohol Use Look Like?

It isn't hard to determine what levels of alcohol consumption are deemed unhealthy. One of the most telling signs is your ability to function as a normal individual without being under the influence of alcohol. If you find yourself incapable of doing everyday tasks without having a drink first, then this should be a cause for concern. From the moment you wake up in the morning till the time you go to bed, your day is filled with all kinds of activities and responsibilities that need 100% of your attention. Going to work and fulfilling your job, parenting your kids and making sure that your family is happy and healthy takes an extreme amount of sacrifice and commitment. If your alcohol consumption affects your work, or your ability to parent and take care of your kids, then you have a problem that should be addressed as soon as possible.

Excessive alcohol consumption really takes a toll on a family, and it has ended many careers and marriages. Most people don't know the signs of alcohol abuse, and they don't even realize that they are headed for disaster. In the next section, we will look at the different signs that you should keep an eye out for because these signs could show that you have an alcohol use disorder.

Warning Signs That Indicate You Have a Serious Drinking Problem

Below, we highlight a list of signs that will help you identify whether you have an actual problem with alcohol. Keep in mind that these signs could differ from person to person, so please make sure that you are aware of these signs in yourself. There is no judgment, as this is done to help you open your eyes to the gravity of the situation.

Common Signs of Alcoholism

- You cannot control how much you drink, and you have no limit. Drinking till you black out often happens, even when you are in the presence of friends or family.
- Whenever you are not drinking, thoughts about alcohol constantly play on your mind. You notice that you physically crave alcohol, and you become anxious without it.
- You place alcohol above your own needs and those of your family. You even start downplaying the importance of spending time

with your family and stop paying attention to them, all because you feel as if you'd rather be drinking.

- After having a few drinks, you feel as if it isn't enough, and it doesn't bring you the same high as before. As a result, you drink more to feel more.

- As your addiction grows, you spend more money on alcohol, and you feel helpless because you cannot cut down. You cut costs in other areas just so that you can afford more alcohol.

- Your friends and family notice a change in your behavior after you've had a few drinks. Even you notice a change in your personality and emotions whenever you drink. This change might seem good for you. However, it could hurt the people who are around you.

- There have been several instances when you have tried to cut down on your drinking but are unsuccessful each time. This shows that you have a serious problem with your drinking.

- Your drinking causes you to slack at work, and you cannot fulfill your responsibilities. Your career takes a hit, as you cannot focus or commit yourself fully the way you used to.

- Your relationship with your spouse deteriorates because you are seeking happiness and comfort in alcohol.

- You notice health issues developing because of your drinking habits. Problems that you hadn't experienced prior to drinking have cropped up now, and you find yourself in a very unhealthy place in your life. You physically cannot do the things you used to do, especially if they require you to be alert and mentally sharp.
- Suddenly, you avoid going out and socializing with people. The only thing that might motivate you to leave the house would be alcohol. If you had to attend an event and there wouldn't be any alcohol present, you would avoid going to that event—for example, school plays, soccer games, and family gatherings or events.
- Feeling nauseous, hands shaking, and body sweats whenever you are not drinking. These are symptoms of withdrawal.

These are the most common signs you should look out for if you suspect you could be addicted to alcohol. Women sometimes feel that having a bottle of wine, or two, daily doesn't lead to you becoming an alcoholic. This couldn't be more untrue. Just because women choose wine as a go-to drink after a hectic day doesn't make it any less of an alcoholic substance. Wine may be considered weak when compared against other drinks such as whiskey or brandy, but this doesn't mean that you can't become addicted to it. Note all the signs that resonate with you from the list provided above. It's important that you be honest with yourself and identify the signs so that you can move forward in this journey to recovery.

What Goes Into One Drink?

We have all heard people say, "Okay, I'll just have one drink," and I'm sure you must have said it as well in your life. But do we understand what goes into one drink? What is the exact amount of alcohol that goes into just one drink? Well, the National Institute of Alcohol Abuse and Alcoholism clearly defines what one drink should include.

- One 350 milliliter bottle or can of beer or cider, that has around five to six percent of alcohol.
- Half a glass of wine, that is around 145 milliliters, with a 12 percent alcohol level.
- Hard liquor, such as brandy and spirits, should be around 44 milliliters, with a 40 percent alcohol level.
- A glass of malt liquor should be around 230–260 milliliters, with a seven percent alcohol

level.

As you can see above, the amount of alcohol that is in one drink could differ depending on the type of alcohol that you are drinking. One beer would not have the same effect on you as one shot of brandy would, and vice versa. Being aware of the different drinks and how much alcohol goes into each one would help you decide on a limit for yourself. People go over their limit, mostly because they don't know how much alcohol they are consuming. You might think that just because you are doing a few shots, there wouldn't be a large amount of alcohol in it, and this is how people end up experiencing blackouts.

When Should You Visit the Doctor?

People always try to avoid visiting a doctor whenever they are feeling unwell. We often blame it on not having enough time or fearing what the doctor might find. However, with alcohol abuse, it would be a good idea to visit your doctor if you notice that your drinking has gotten out of hand. The same goes if your family cannot handle your behavior whenever you drink and they are concerned about your health. Consider seeing a mental health professional who will help you overcome your addiction. One important thing to remember: there is no shame in seeking help. It takes someone courageous to admit to their mistakes and to ask for help. This doesn't make you weak, or paint you in a poor light in front of others. Don't let shame and embarrassment hold you back from doing what is best for you and your family. It can be incredibly difficult to take this step, especially when you know you will be required to give up drinking alcohol once and for all. If you are not ready to do that, the fear of losing alcohol could hold you back from seeking the help that you so desperately need.

The Science Behind Alcohol Cravings

Alcohol cravings can show up unannounced during the day. Almost anything can trigger it, from loud music playing at your next-door neighbor's party to having a slice of fruitcake that tastes ever so strong and pungent. You wouldn't even have the slightest clue that you are craving alcohol. So what is the science behind alcohol cravings? Let's take a deeper look at how cravings work. First things first; you must understand that alcohol is a drug. It has the power to alter a person's emotions and ability to decide clearly. When you consume alcohol, it directly affects the glutamate system, which is a system of neurological pathways in the brain. Alcohol is a stimulant and a depressant, which accounts for the changes in mood and behavior seen when it's consumed.

Prolonged exposure to alcohol could alter the glutamate system, resulting in an increase in cravings. The more alcohol you consume, the more intense your cravings will be. Your brain becomes re-wired because of excessive alcohol use, and this changes your moods and your ability to control your cravings. Even the slightest taste or smell of alcohol could set off alarm bells ringing in your brain. This can make it harder for people who are recovering from addiction. No one can deny that a fun-filled night out with the girls will always be a splendid memory that you will cherish. The way you danced, the drinks you had, and the smell of the night air, these things will be a part of that memory. These memories ultimately trigger your cravings for alcohol, causing you to want to relive that night with your friends by drinking.

Complications of Alcohol Abuse

Alcohol can affect your life in so many ways. It can affect your physical and emotional well-being, as well as your relationships and your career. Because you are under the influence of alcohol regularly, you wouldn't be able to see how badly it can affect your life. Below, we inspect how alcohol abuse can cause complications in different areas of your life.

How Does Alcohol Abuse Impact Your Health?

The impact alcohol has on the human body is unbelievable. It is a powerful substance that has the potential to cause death if a person consumes too much at once. The body cannot regulate high levels of alcohol in one go, thus leading to alcohol poisoning, which then results in death. Your alcohol consumption affects every organ in your body. You might not see it or feel it, but that doesn't mean the damage is not being done. Let's look at how alcohol affects your health negatively.

▷ Cardiovascular Problems

Consuming large amounts of alcohol on a regular basis puts you at risk of developing high blood pressure and other heart-related issues. Excessive alcohol consumption has caused heart enlargement, which leads to strokes and heart failure in people. Just one binge of alcohol could cause the heart to develop irregular heartbeats, also known as arrhythmia or atrial fibrillation. When a person drinks a large amount of alcohol, it places an exorbitant amount of stress on the heart to work overtime to support the organs in the body while they are regulating the high levels of alcohol out of the system. This constant strain can really affect the heart in dangerous ways, and if the heart cannot function properly, then the rest of the organs will shut down.

▷ Liver Issues

Excessive alcohol consumption can lead to the liver becoming enlarged and inflamed (alcoholic hepatitis). The liver accumulates fat because of the constant amount of alcohol that is being processed, and this leads to hepatic steatosis. These complications cause irreversible damage and scarring to the liver, which only adds to the severe health conditions. The majority of alcoholic people die from liver-related issues, because of excessive drinking that they cannot break free from. Your liver processes the alcohol you consume and makes sure that your body eliminates all toxins that might be introduced to the body through alcohol. Constant drinking will affect the liver negatively, resulting in serious health complications.

▷ Digestive Complications

Your stomach is a very sensitive organ that digests the food and liquids that you consume. The lining of the stomach can become irritated and inflamed when exposed to alcohol frequently. This causes gastritis, which also leads to the individual developing ulcers in the esophagus and in the stomach. When this happens, your intestines cannot absorb the vitamins and nutrients from the foods you eat. You will feel full after eating small amounts, and you will experience mild to severe stomach cramps. Nausea and vomiting develops because of ulcers, which are also known as stomach sores. Your digestive system gets thrown off track because of the outrageous amount of alcohol you consume. Symptoms worsen when alcohol is consumed on an empty stomach.

▷ **Diabetes**

Certain types of alcohol are high in sugar, and if consumed frequently, it could lead to diabetes in many individuals. Apart from that, alcohol also interferes with how your liver produces and releases glucose, which can increase the risk of low blood sugar. Now, if you are a person who has diabetes, drinking large amounts of alcohol could be dangerous for your health. Having a drink occasionally wouldn't cause much reason for concern. However, daily consumption of alcohol could cause further complications to your health as a diabetic.

▷ **Menstrual Cycle and Your Sex Life**

For men, excessive drinking could lead to problems with their sex life because alcohol could cause erectile dysfunction. It is medically proven that men who consume large amounts of alcohol experience problems in their sex life (Mayo Clinic, 2018). When it comes to women, frequent consumption of alcohol can affect the menstrual cycle, causing irregular periods with heavier flows. After drinking for a prolonged period, fertility issues could arise because of the menstrual cycle not being normal. In some women, alcohol decreases sex drive, making them feel less sexy and out of touch with their bodies.

▷ Eyesight Issues

Believe it or not, alcohol can cause problems with your eyes. Involuntary eye movements, also known as nystagmus, occur because of excessive drinking. Alcohol decreases the amount of vitamin B in your body, which can cause your eye muscles to weaken and become paralyzed. Along with this, your eyesight would also deteriorate over time, with no hope of correction in the future. Also, hangovers cause intense headaches that also affect your ability to see properly.

▷ Defects in Unborn Babies

Women who consume alcohol during their pregnancy place their developing babies at risk for developing fetal alcohol syndrome. This causes birth defects that change the physical appearance of these babies and damages their developing brains, which causes lifetime intellectual disability and therefore no chance of independent living. Once these babies are born, life becomes hard, as they are born with withdrawal symptoms as well. A baby can become addicted to alcohol while in the womb. As the mother continues to drink throughout her pregnancy, she is also causing her baby to develop a dependency on alcohol.

▷ Neurological Issues

Your brain can become intensely affected by the amount of alcohol that you consume. This also affects your central nervous system, causing pain and numbness in your limbs. Your thought process is also disrupted, which decreases your ability to make well-constructed decisions. Excessive alcohol consumption also leads to dementia and memory loss in many people. The effects of alcohol on the brain are so severe that it can even alter a person's personality, changing them into a whole other individual.

▷ Bone Health Issues

Throughout our lifetime, our body continuously produces new bones to compensate for the thinning of our old bones. Alcohol can affect the bone production process, haltering the body's ability to replace old bone with new bone. This can cause osteoporosis, a bone disease, which results in an increased risk for fractures and broken bones. Alcohol even affects the bone marrow, which creates blood cells. When this happens, your body will be more prone to becoming bruised easily because of the low blood cell count.

▷ Immune System Becomes Weaker

Your immune system fights off many illnesses and diseases that invade the body. By drinking excessively, you automatically compromise your immune system, and you leave yourself vulnerable to disease and illnesses. Because your body is spending so much time and resources trying to help you recover from every alcohol binge, it doesn't have any extra resources or time to fight off other illnesses that may occur suddenly. The immune system thrives when the body and mind are healthy and in tune together. When your immune system is happy and well-rested, it will protect your body the way it should.

▷ Cancer

Long-term alcohol consumption leads to an increased risk of cancer of the mouth, liver, throat, breast, and colon. Most women put themselves at an increased risk of breast cancer when they consume alcohol frequently. Since alcohol use causes your body's immune system to weaken, cancer cells can multiply rapidly. Without the body's defense system ready to attack and hijack cancer cells, they have the opportunity to grow at a rapid pace.

▷ Taking Medication and Drinking Alcohol

Drinking alcohol when taking prescribed medication can be a toxic mix that could cause serious health complications for an individual. Alcohol could either alter the effects of these medications or render them useless and unable to serve their purpose. Hence, doctors always warn against consuming alcohol while taking certain medications. It can lead to drowsiness and impairment, which isn't safe when driving and taking care of your kids.

▷ Prevention

As the famous saying goes, prevention is better than cure. This is very true for alcohol abuse. Trying your best to prevent addiction is a thousand times better than being in recovery. However, most people wouldn't already be addicted to alcohol if prevention was possible for them. But if you are one of those people who caught on early, then you can take steps to prevent yourself from becoming a full-blown alcoholic. For most people, it can be difficult to see the signs in themselves, so it would be a good idea if you could speak to a trusted family member or friend who can point out whether you have an unhealthy relationship with alcohol. If you do display any of the signs mentioned, then it could very well show that your relationship with alcohol may destroy your life. This is the moment where you decide to take action and set things right. You can prevent things from getting any worse.

A Word About Denial

Denial is a common symptom of alcoholism. It is a psychological reaction to pain, stress, or conflict. We all have done it at some point in our lives, and there is no judgment involved here. Many people suffering from alcoholism refuse to admit the truth or reality of the situation. Being in denial keeps you from seeking the help that you need and taking control of your life. It's important to accept the truth, no matter how painful or embarrassing it can be. Everyone has a different view of their relationship with alcohol. Some people would have realized by now the seriousness of their situation, while others may still be trying to understand their relationship with alcohol.

Why Do People Deny Their Problems With Alcohol?

There are several reasons people choose to deny that they have a problem with alcohol. It could be because they don't even realize that they have a problem. When someone cannot identify the problem within themselves, you cannot expect them to accept what everyone else is telling them. They would have to see it for themselves first. Honestly, if you don't see that you have a problem with alcohol, you would never listen to the advice that other people are giving you. Another reason people deny their addiction to alcohol is that they are afraid of being judged by others. The shame and embarrassment would be too much to bear, so they hide their problems instead.

Another reason for denial is the fear of change. Human beings are creatures of habit. We like things to be done a certain way, and we become accustomed to living our lives in a way that benefits us to the max. Opening up about an alcohol use disorder would mean that you have to change to overcome that issue. That profound change could mean losing friends that have been a bad influence in your life, or moving to another state and starting off fresh, or even going to rehab for a few months to help you recover from alcohol addiction. These are tremendous changes that require you to move out of habit and embrace a new chapter of your life. This can bring about feelings of agonizing fear and anxiety. Most people deny that they have a drinking problem, mainly because they fear being judged or rejected by their family and friends. No one wants to experience rejection, especially when they need all the love and support they can get in order to recover from their issues with alcohol.

Opening up and accepting that you have a problem places you in a vulnerable position, and when you are vulnerable, that's when you could get hurt the most. This brings us to another reason people don't admit to their drinking problems. They fear getting hurt, and because they are not in a good place emotionally or mentally, they wouldn't be able to handle the pain of being ostracized from their family and friends. It would push them further into addiction, so they choose to live in denial for as long as they can. Another reason people deny that they have trouble with drinking alcohol is pride and ego. They don't want to be embarrassed or looked down upon by others, and they understand that once people find out about their alcohol abuse, they would lose respect in society, in their jobs, and with their families.

The only way to avoid this is by avoiding the truth and pretending that you are okay. Whatever the reasons, denial will hold you back from the brighter future that you can achieve for yourself. You have already taken a gigantic step on your journey to recovery. This is commendable, and I applaud you for being open to the process. You don't realize it, but you have already come so far. Continue on this journey with me as we explore why alcohol is so addictive.

Different Forms of Denial

Denial comes in many forms, and it isn't too hard to notice when someone is in denial. Below, I've listed the different forms of denial. Because people are different and share their own experiences with alcohol abuse, they might display different forms of denial. However, try to focus on yourself when going over these forms of denial, so that you can identify if you might express your denial in any of the following ways.

▷ Rationalization

A person who has an alcohol disorder might try to justify their mistakes and destructive behavior by providing reasonable excuses. They would say things like, "The fight didn't happen because I was drinking; it happened because I was upset." Trying to rationalize a situation that has occurred only because of the drinking is one form of denial that many people fall into.

▷ Shifting Blame

Blaming other people or situations is one of the most common forms of denial. A person with an alcoholic disorder would try to shift blame onto another person and would avoid accepting fault for their behavior and mistakes. They would say, "If you didn't take me to the bar with you tonight, none of this would have happened."

▷ Dishonesty

When a person fears being judged by those around them, they will hide the truth about their problems with alcohol. Being truthful and forthcoming about your relationship with alcohol is a tough thing to do. And when people aren't ready to face it, they will be dishonest, and make up lies about where they've been and what they've been doing.

▷ Being Defensive

As soon as the subject of alcohol is mentioned, they would become defensive and closed off from the conversation. If someone directed a question about alcohol towards you, for example, you would do everything possible to deflect that question back at the other person, saying things like, "I didn't drink today! You're always making me seem like an alcoholic."

▷ Comparing Your Drinking Problems With Others

This is another common form of denial. Because they want to normalize their drinking issues, they would compare their situation or behavior to others. They think that if they bring another person's wrongdoings to light, it will make their own situation seem insignificant. They would say things like, "Sarah ended up in hospital because of her excessive drinking. She had an accident while driving drunk. If I had a drinking problem, I would have ended up in the hospital as well."

▷ Dismissive Behavior

Talking about alcohol with someone who clearly has a drinking problem would cause them to become dismissive of everything you say to them. They would try to downplay all of your concerns with statements like, "Don't stress yourself about it; it isn't a big issue." They would always say things that would switch you off and make it seem like you are overthinking things.

▷ Avoiding the Issue

The most famous form of denial would avoid the problem altogether. Whenever a question is asked about alcohol, they would beat around the bush and change the topic a hundred times, but they would never give you a straight answer to your questions. They would even walk away from the discussion just so that they can avoid being asked questions about their relationship with alcohol.

MAIN REASONS FOR ALCOHOL ABUSE

As mentioned previously, there is no set reason why alcoholics drink; it all boils down to personal reasons. If you had to interact daily with someone who has an alcohol disorder, it would be very hard for you to determine what their reasons are for drinking. They would not readily share this information with people because it isn't something that they are proud of. However, a few of the reasons people drink are most common around the world. There are several risk factors that come into play which make certain people more prone to alcoholism. Addiction usually starts during a person's late 20s and early 30s; however, this could differ between individuals. Let's take a look at some of the risk factors that are associated with alcohol addiction.

▷ **Reason 1: Genetic Predisposition**

Alcoholism typically runs in the family. If you have a parent or family member who had problems with alcohol, chances are that your troubles with addiction could have stemmed from that. There are genetic factors that come into play. However, growing up around people who drank a lot is enough to influence your relationship with alcohol. As a child, if you see a family member using alcohol as a coping mechanism, then that would automatically rub off on you. Whenever you encounter difficult situations as an adult, you would resort to alcohol to help you get through those tough times. It can be hard not to follow in the footsteps of your family when you are exposed to these things from a young, impressionable age. In 2008, the NIAAA (National Institute on Alcohol Abuse and Alcoholism) carried out a study. This study showed that there was a 40–60 percent chance of people becoming addicted to alcohol because of genetics (*Why Do Alcoholics Drink? 4 Reasons behind Alcohol Abuse*, 2020).

Believe it or not, your genes can play a huge role in your relationship with alcohol. Because your family members had problems with alcohol, your chances of developing an alcohol disorder would be greater than someone who didn't have a family history of alcoholism. There are certain genes that run in the family, and these genes can heighten your experience with alcohol, depending on how well the body metabolizes it. Some people refrain from alcohol because they don't always have a pleasant experience with it. They may feel nauseated, flustered, and their moods could be irregular. However, other people who drink would feel euphoric and happy because of their genes, and these people are more likely to develop an alcoholic disorder.

▷ Reason 2: Chemical Imbalance in the Brain

The brain is a complex organ in the body, and it handles all our decision-making abilities. There are neurotransmitters in our brains which regulate our emotions and process information. When you drink alcohol, it increases levels of serotonin in the brain, and this handles our "feel good" emotions. This motivates you to keep drinking so that you can continue to feel good. It also decreases the chemicals in the brain that process information, so whenever you drink, you wouldn't be caught up in your thoughts and feelings of sadness. The more alcohol you drink, the more you compromise your brain's ability to think clearly and make sound decisions. This chemical imbalance does more harm than good, and in most cases, it takes a long time for the damage to be reversed. Chasing that feeling of pleasure and reward will ultimately cost you your peace of mind.

▷ Reason 3: Drinking From an Early Age

People who have drunk alcohol from a young age are more likely to develop issues with it when they become adults. Most people experiment with alcohol when they are around 15 or 16 years old. Boys are more likely to drink earlier than girls, and this usually happens during their high school years. High school and college students throw a lot of parties where alcohol is readily available to anyone who wants to try it out. When I was 17 years old, I started drinking. I was young; I didn't understand the full effects of alcohol. But from the moment I tried it, I became drawn to that feeling, that buzz that takes you away from reality. And because I experienced that feeling at a young age when I didn't know better, it led to me becoming an alcoholic in my early adult years.

▷ **Reason 4: Experiencing Trauma**

This is one of the primary risk factors that leads to people, especially women, becoming addicted to alcohol. What is trauma? We can classify trauma as a negative experience that causes immense fear, pain, shock, and long-term anxiety in a person. Trauma can stem from sexual abuse, physical abuse, emotional abuse, or from the death and loss of a loved one. When an event shocks you to your core and plunges you into a dark place, that can push you into developing an alcohol disorder. Living with feelings of anger, guilt, shame, and regret is never easy, especially if you're a woman who has been through a situation that has stripped you of dignity and self-respect. Alcohol would seem like a quick fix that could erase the memories and make life bearable, as long as you are under the influence. But when you wake up the next morning, you are back to square one with all the traumatic memories and feelings flooding back.

▷ Reason 5: Anxiety and Depression

Mental health problems have been related to excessive alcohol use in both men and women all over the world. Because alcohol has properties that calms and relaxes you, people who have issues with anxiety and depression often abuse it. Living with these mental health disorders can be challenging. There is no happiness, hope, excitement, or desire to live life and be adventurous when you are experiencing depression. Instead, you feel you are constantly on edge, stressed about the little things, unable to be present in the moment and feel content. Alcohol provides relief, to a certain degree, for people who are depressed. Although it cannot make them feel true happiness, it places them in a euphoric state, which simulates being happy. For people with anxiety disorders, alcohol can be both a blessing and a curse. It can help them be calmer and less anxious, but when they are trying to recover from addiction, the cravings can worsen anxiety.

Because alcohol seemingly makes life more bearable and easier, it becomes a crutch for people with mental health issues. This is one of the major reasons why people cannot give up their addiction to alcohol. For some people, alcohol works better than certain medica-

ALCOHOL RECOVERY FOR WOMEN | 43

tions used to treat mental health conditions. However, the side effects of using alcohol to treat mental health are damaging in the long run. It cannot be used as a treatment or as a cure for your depression and anxiety. Most people are ashamed of taking medication for their mental health because they think that they will be deemed crazy by their friends and family.

▷ **Reason 6: Horrible Withdrawal Symptoms**

Withdrawal symptoms from prolonged alcohol abuse can be nasty, to say the least. Most people continue drinking because they don't want to face withdrawal. Some symptoms of alcohol withdrawal include nausea, intense headaches, body chills, mood swings, anxiety, depression, vomiting, and in severe cases, seizures. These symptoms are scary enough to make a person continue drinking. Overcoming withdrawal takes a strong mindset and a reliable support system. Without these two components, it would be very difficult to face withdrawal alone. You will need the support and encouragement of family and friends to see you through the withdrawal phase. People who don't have the support of their own families need to seek help from rehab centers to get them through the withdrawal phase.

▷ Reason 7: The Need for Pleasure and Happiness

Once the brain becomes accustomed to the pleasures that alcohol brings, it will automatically tell the body that you have to drink more, if you want to experience feelings of pleasure. The normal things in life that are supposed to bring you happiness, such as spending time with your kids, or going on a date, or joking around with your friends, these things won't have a strong enough effect on your brain to make you feel happy the way alcohol does. This is due to the fact that your brain will only respond to alcohol because you've become conditioned to think it's the only thing that makes you feel pleasure.

▷ Reason 8: Positive Advertising

There are so many advertisements out there that paint alcohol in a good light. Seeing these ads would only derail the progress of a recovering addict because they are portraying how fun alcohol is. Yes, people can enjoy alcohol without becoming addicted to it, and these ads are aimed at promoting that idea. However, it can be difficult for those people who have issues with alcohol addiction. These advertisements are available online, on social media apps, in newspapers and magazines, billboards and on TV. They can be hard to avoid, and someone with an alcohol disorder will feel like drinking every time they see these ads.

▷ **Reason 9: Living Close to Bars and Liquor stores**

When alcohol is readily available, at any time, it can be unbearably difficult to avoid it. Living close to bars and liquor stores will only make your recovery harder. Also, if your family members drink alcohol regularly, and if it's always lying around the house, this will fuel your desire to carry on drinking because alcohol is always available. Going out with your friends to a place where alcohol will be served, is equally tempting as having it lying around the house. Even if you wake up one day and decide to give up alcohol, your decision could be swayed every time.

▷ **Reason 10: Being Influenced by Friends and Peers**

There are thousands of people who started off their tumultuous relationship with alcohol through being influenced by friends or work colleagues. Teenagers as young as 14 years old experiment with alcohol, mainly because their friends urge them to do so. They want to be a part of the group, and they don't want to come across as being uncool, so they get involved with alcohol without fully being aware of the consequences of their actions. Fueled by their desire to fit in and be accepted, teenagers can easily fall into addiction because of their excessive alcohol consumption. Apart from teenagers, adults are also easily influenced by their friends as well. Everyone wants to be socially accepted, and consuming alcohol is a big part of society these days. If you have a few drinks every time you go out with your friends, you are unknowingly setting yourself up to become addicted to alcohol.

Jean's Story of Alcohol Abuse

Jean was known as the life of the party. She knew how to have fun, and she loved making others laugh. Jean is a recovering alcoholic who was lucky enough to survive to share her story. She started drinking from a young age, and she became popular in high school because she could always out-drink her friends. Her drinking continued through high school and college and lasted throughout her first job. She worked at a law office, but she still managed to go out drinking every night and go to work the next day. Jean was married a couple of times, and she had held some top positions in her career. She worked at prestigious law firms, a governor's office, state senator's office, and the list goes on. Although she drank a lot, she still managed to achieve success in her career. Jean's drinking got out of hand. Her last husband kicked her out of the house and divorced her. He took the children with him, leaving Jean alone and without any support.

That's when Jean started drinking more and more until she started experiencing blackouts. She started blaming everyone else for her drinking problems; she even blamed the death of one of her children. She looked at the blackouts as some sort of blessing, because she could no longer tolerate the pain when she was sober. Eventually, there came a time when she could no longer attend work and hold down a job. She had to have a drink every few hours, and this could not happen if she was working. Jean had hit rock bottom when she realized that she didn't have money for rent or for food, and she was left with nothing but a quarter. She didn't have anyone there to help her, as her family was using the "tough love" approach on her. She finally decided to call AA (Alcoholics Anonymous) so that she could get her drinking under control. AA helped Jane clean up her act, and after a year of being sober, Jean made another mistake. She thought that she could handle being a social drinker. But little did she know that trouble was around the corner.

After she had experienced another blackout, Jean decided that enough was enough and that she was going to reclaim her sobriety. Even though she messed up, she believed in herself. She knew that she could get back to that place of being sober. And so she did; her family stood by her and supported her through it. Jean was proud of herself as she collected her 17-year sobriety chip. She spent most of her life being drunk and living for alcohol, but today Jean lives for herself. She had lost so much because of her alcohol disorder, but she didn't let that keep her from rebuilding her life. Yes, she did hit a few speed bumps and backslid just when she was making progress. But she managed to set herself straight back onto the right path.

In Closing

Just like Jean, you have a chance to reclaim your power as a woman. You might have spent a lot of time thinking about what life would be like if only you could overcome this alcohol addiction. Now you don't have to wonder anymore. You can make it a reality, and you can live your life free from the tight grip of alcohol. You might have lost your family or your job. Maybe your health took a hit because of drinking. But I'm here to tell you that it's never too late to make a change. This chapter has taught you about the complications of long-term alcohol use, it has helped you understand the science beyond addiction, and it has opened your eyes to denial. Now is the time to put what you have learned into practice. Use this knowledge to help you on your journey to recovery. In the next chapter, we will be focusing on step one of the recovery process. Open up your mind and your heart, and surrender yourself completely to this journey. No matter how many times you fail, you can always start again and again.

2

STEP 1: TRY TO UNDERSTAND YOURSELF

UNDERSTANDING WHERE YOU ARE IN ADDICTION

In this chapter, you will dig deeper inside yourself to try to find out the main reasons that fuel your relationship with alcohol. You are going to learn how to understand yourself better to bring out your best side. You have to get into the right mindset to welcome change, and the only way this can happen is if you are honest with yourself and face your fears. The innermost painful truths, which you have kept hidden for all this while, have to be embraced so that you can move forward in your journey. You cannot recover fully if you don't address the real-life issues that are holding you captive in this relationship with alcohol. Getting in touch with who you truly are is the most important aspect of recovery, and I am here to help you and guide you through it all.

In the previous chapter, we discussed the reasons why people drink. You must have also understood your reasons for drinking, whether it was because of an incident that happened in your life that you are trying to get over, or that your drinking has more to do with family history and genetics. Whatever your reasons, you now have to determine why you want to give up drinking. This is what is most important during this stage of your recovery. Identifying what stage of alcoholism you are in will help you work on a suitable recovery plan.

Stages of Alcoholism

There are different stages to alcoholism, and the majority of the time, people don't realize exactly where they stand. If you had to ask yourself right now about what stage of alcoholism, you think you are in, there would probably be a lot of confusion involved in your answer. This is completely normal; however, it is crucial that you identify how serious your alcohol disorder has become so that you can take the necessary steps to recover successfully. A lot of the time, people fail on their journey because they are not being 100% honest with themselves about the severity of their drinking. You can save yourself a lot of time and hard work, if only you can be fully honest with yourself at the start of your journey.

▷ **Stage 1: Pre-Alcoholic**

This is the initial stage of alcoholism, where the person drinks mainly to feel better about themselves. They want to drink to forget their pain, or to stop worrying about certain issues in their life. They do still have control over their drinking at this point, because they choose to drink when they cannot handle their emotions. If not properly managed, their drinking can escalate quite fast after this stage.

▷ **Stage 2: Early Alcoholic**

During this stage, blackouts occur more frequently. That is how you identify that your relationship with alcohol is getting out of hand. Drinking to the point where you black out gives the indication that you are losing control with alcohol. You find yourself walking a fine line, where you have to decide whether you are controlling alcohol or if alcohol is controlling you. Even at this stage, you would still think that you are in control, which makes it harder for you to see that you have a problem.

▷ **Stage 3: Middle Alcoholic**

At this stage, your relationship with alcohol is clear for everyone to see. Your family and friends would have noticed, by now, that you have a drinking problem. There would be times when you would miss work or forget to pick your kids up from school, and you would just be so moody and irritated whenever you didn't drink. Your physical appearance changes a lot during this stage. You might lose some weight, or gain it, depending on how your body reacts to alcohol. You would also lose interest in your clothes and neglect yourself because of drinking all the time.

▷ **Stage 4: Late Alcoholic**

When you have reached this stage, drinking becomes the number one priority in your life. From the moment you wake up, till you go to bed, all you think about is getting another drink. You begin to neglect your family, you even quit your job, and you would spend your last money on a bottle. At this stage, you have lost all control over your drinking, and you can no longer function on a normal level unless you are under the influence of alcohol. Whenever you try to stop drinking, you experience withdrawal symptoms that become too much to handle.

Once you have determined what stage of alcoholism you are in, you can then work on a recovery plan with your doctor. It takes a lot of courage to admit that you are a middle alcoholic or a late alcoholic. I appreciate that you are taking steps to try and figure out where you stand in your relationship with alcohol. Don't feel ashamed to admit that you have a problem, because acceptance is key to making a change. If you are not willing to accept that you have a serious problem, then you will not be willing to put in the work that is required of you. Remember that your friends and family, who point out that you have a drinking problem, are not doing it to embarrass you. They are speaking up because they are concerned about you, and they want you to take responsibility for your decisions and actions. Now is the time to address your problems with alcohol.

Think About Your Reasons for Quitting

Having a clear understanding of why you want to quit alcohol is paramount to the recovery process. Now is the time for you to do some soul-searching. Question your intentions behind wanting to give up on drinking alcohol. It can be difficult to do this on your own, especially if you are under the influence of alcohol. Below, we provide you with some tips to help you through the process of figuring out exactly why you want to quit drinking.

▷ **Work With a Counselor or Therapist**

Giving up alcohol is never an easy decision to make. It would be a good idea to work with a medical professional, such as a therapist or counselor, who will be able to guide you along the process. Working with a therapist will be beneficial in figuring out why you want to give up drinking alcohol. They can help you work through your emotions, and schedule sessions when you aren't under the influence of alcohol. Having a clear mind is important when thinking about why you want to free yourself from addiction. Working with someone also gives you accountability and makes you feel more obligated to put in the hard work. Knowing that you have to answer to someone will make the process much more successful than if you were working on your own.

▷ **Keep a Journal**

Writing your feelings down in a journal can be extremely helpful in determining how you truly feel about alcohol. Whether you are under the influence of alcohol, or whether you are sober, you can write in your journal anytime. Reading back on what you have written will help you see where your head's at. A journal can help you keep track of your thoughts and emotions, without having to share them with others. Your innermost thoughts and desires can be expressed in this book, with the main purpose of helping you understand yourself a bit more. When our thoughts are on paper, it becomes much easier to understand them than if they were circling around in our minds.

▷ Have an Intervention

The final thing a person with an alcohol use disorder needs is an intervention. When family and friends plan interventions, it always surprises the person in question because they would never agree to attend an intervention. However, this is necessary when you decide to give up on alcohol. Arrange for your family and friends to come and visit, because their opinions can help you see how bad the problem is. Ask them to be open and honest about their feelings regarding your relationship with alcohol. Try not to be defensive or stand-offish when they give their opinions about you. Accept it, and acknowledge what they have to say because it is vital that you see the bigger picture. An intervention could help you face the truth in a safe place with your family and friends around you to offer their support.

▷ Seek Guidance From Your Spiritual Head

If you believe in God, and you follow a specific religion or faith, then it would benefit you to seek the help and guidance of your spiritual head. It could be your pastor, a priest, a shaman, or a guru. Whatever your faith may be, these spiritual heads could help you dig deep inside yourself and find the answers to your questions. They will provide you with clarity on why you want to give up alcohol. Having hope and faith is an essential part of your recovery process, and knowing that there is a higher power up there to guide you would provide so much comfort to your soul.

Focus on the Benefits

If you don't have a specific reason that contributes to your desire to quit alcohol, then the best thing you could do is focus on the benefits of quitting. There are several life-changing benefits that you will reap when you stop drinking alcohol. These benefits will help motivate you to stop drinking alcohol. I'm sure you have desires and goals you want to attain in life. Once you quit alcohol and start your life afresh, you can achieve these goals. Let's look at all the benefits you will gain once you quit alcohol. Keep an open mind and believe that these things can happen to you.

▷ Your Relationships Will Improve

Once you quit drinking alcohol, your relationships will start to improve significantly. The relationships you share with your friends and family can heal when you turn your life around. When people drink, they become selfish and uncontrollable. This can cause the people you love to walk away from you. Marriages end in divorce, kids get taken away, friendships break apart, and family rejects you because of your toxic relationship with alcohol. You do have a chance at repairing these relationships, but you can only do it if you are completely sober. You can have a relationship with your kids again, you can try to fix your broken marriage if your partner is willing, and you can rebuild the friendships you lost. Your family and friends expect you to take responsibility for your life and make the right choices, and once you get sober, you will be able to pursue these relationships and fix whatever was broken, and allow happiness to flow again. You can even build new relationships, make new friends and find a new partner to spend the rest of your life with.

▷ You Can Rebuild Your Career

Alcohol must have robbed you of many things that meant a lot to you. Things that made you who you are, like your job or career for example. Chasing the high that alcohol brings means you have to constantly drink more and more to obtain the same feeling. There is no way you could still hold a job in that condition, which would have led to you losing your job or ruining your business. However, as devastating as that might have been, I'm here to tell you that it's not the end. You can rebuild your business from the ground up. You can find another job and start off with a clean slate. It will take some hard work and commitment, but you can get everything back. You can become the professional you were before. People will still respect you and want to work with you, especially after hearing your story and how you overcame addiction.

▷ Re-Learn Skills and Further Your Education

All the skills that you have acquired throughout the years would have diminished because of the effects that alcohol had on your brain. When you do not put your skills to use for long periods of time, they begin to wilt away. Maybe your greatest skills were being computer savvy or cake decorating. These skills require a high level of concentration and hand coordination to be done successfully. Long-term alcohol use leads to body shakes and decreased alertness in your mind. You forget things easily, and it can even reach a point where almost half of your life is blacked out because of excessive alcohol use. It may seem as if you can never be the same person you were before, because all the things that made you whom you were have now disappeared. But if you give up alcohol, you can re-learn those skills and become even better at it. You even have the opportunity to further your studies and complete a new course. Life doesn't stop after addiction.

Incredible Health Benefits to Look Forward To

This might sound surprising to you, but there are amazing health benefits to look forward to once you stop drinking alcohol. Your body will start to heal itself when the alcohol has left your system once and for all. People with have alcohol disorders often think that their health has been ruined for the rest of their lives. Even if you have developed complications that cannot be reversed due to excessive drinking, you could still improve your overall health, which would ease your symptoms and allow you to do things you couldn't do before. Here are some excellent health benefits that you can look forward to now that you have decided to quit drinking.

▷ Improved Brain Health

You now have an understanding of how excessive alcohol drinking can affect your brain. This means that you lose the ability to think clearly, speak clearly, and understand what is going on around you. In spite of these negative side effects of alcohol, your brain health can improve significantly when you cut down on your alcohol consumption. As time progresses, you will gain back the ability to make clear decisions and your memory will also improve. The dark layer of fog that covered your brain will disappear, and you will start noticing things about your life that you hadn't paid attention to previously.

▷ More Energy

The more alcohol you drink, the more dehydrated your body becomes. When your body is dehydrated, you don't have much energy to do the things you normally would. That is why people who drink are overwhelmed by chores, such as cleaning their home or keeping themselves neat. They just don't have the energy to maintain their homes or to look after themselves. This could all change when you cut off your ties with alcohol. Your energy levels will improve tremendously when alcohol is no longer in your system. The body will heal and rehydrate itself the natural way. This means more energy to do the things you have to do.

▷ Your Heart Gets Healthier

Lowering your alcohol consumption, or quitting altogether, significantly lowers your blood pressure and decreases your chances of heart failure. Your heart works harder when you are constantly drinking alcohol. This places a lot of strain on the heart muscle, which increases the risk of heart attacks. But once you stop drinking, your heart has a chance to recover and become healthier. Arrhythmia may reduce, and your heart will settle into a regular rhythm of its own without having additional stress from alcohol.

▷ The Liver Can Heal

Your liver's main job is to filter toxins out from your blood and get rid of them. Alcohol interferes with the liver's ability to do this, and toxins begin to build up in the body as a result. Excessive alcohol consumption could lead to all kinds of problems with the liver, such as cirrhosis. However, your liver can heal from all the drinking, if you give yourself a chance to give it up. Your liver can repair itself, and undo most of the damage that has been caused by alcohol. It might take some time, but it is possible. Your liver can get back to a place of being healthy, and the only way that is going to happen is if you give up on drinking. The amount of fat that surrounds your liver will be reduced significantly (Roerecke et al., 2019).

▷ You Can Take Control of Your Weight

Alcohol contains a lot of calories, and when paired with unhealthy eating habits, you could gain a fair amount of weight each week. However, this is not the case for everyone. Some people could gain weight because of their unhealthy relationship with alcohol, and others could lose weight because of it. You can regain control of your body and manage your weight better. Once you get the alcohol out of your system, your body will be fit enough to follow a balanced diet. Exercise can also become a part of your daily routine, which is a great way to keep you at a healthy weight. It takes a lot of mental power to focus on a weight loss plan, and your mind will be able to do this only when you aren't under the influence of alcohol.

▷ Lower Your Risk of Cancer

To lower your risk of cancer, you will need to cut off the alcohol for good. Alcohol can drastically increase your risk of developing different types of cancer in your body. As mentioned previously, your body would not be healthy enough to fight off cancer when you are drinking excessively. Cancer can show up unannounced, and knowing that you are at risk because of alcohol abuse would only add to your frustrations. Even though cancer can happen to anyone, young or old, alcoholic or not, it isn't wise to increase your risks by drinking excessively. Give yourself a chance to make the right decisions for your health (Scoccianti et al., 2014).

▷ Your Sex Life Will Improve

With alcoholism comes a range of different health issues, including those that affect your sex life. As a woman, your sex life would be greatly impacted by the amount of alcohol you drink daily. While a drink or two might help you feel more sexually free, drinking excessively can have an adverse effect on your sex drive. This issue can be reversed when you quit drinking alcohol. As your physical health improves, so, too, will your sexual health get better. You can prepare yourself to get back in the game and enjoy a healthy sex life with your partner. It is an important part of a relationship, and it does help you maintain that bond with your significant other. Excessive drinking decreases your sex drive and kills your interest in sex, which can cause problems in marriages and relationships. You can help heal your relationship; quitting alcohol does make a difference.

▷ Better Absorption of Vitamins and Minerals

Alcohol makes it difficult for your body to absorb much-needed nutrients from the foods we consume. You can eat the best foods, stay away from fats and artificial sugars, and it wouldn't make a difference because the moment you have your first drink for the day, it jeopardizes your ability to harvest these important nutrients from your food. How will you function as a healthy human being without these vitamins? The great news is that this isn't a permanent problem. As soon as you stop drinking alcohol, your body would be better positioned to absorb nutrients from your food. You might need the help of Vitamins C supplement to help you get started, but once your body recovers fully, you will reap the benefits of eating healthily.

▷ **Good Night's Rest**

This is a health benefit that you must be looking forward to. Getting a good night's rest would have been next to impossible during your time as an alcoholic. Now, you may be thinking that much of the time you were blacked out; however, blacking out every night from excessive drinking isn't a form of rest. When you give up alcohol, you might have trouble sleeping for the first few days. But once the alcohol is completely gone from your system, you will finally experience rest as you did before. Your mind, your body, and your soul needs rest so that you can function at your best every day. This will become your reality; all you have to do is say goodbye to alcohol.

▷ **Amazing Skin**

Have you noticed how dry and dull your skin has been because of drinking? Alcohol is packed with toxins that literally suck the life out of you, dehydrating the body.

This causes the skin to become dry and wrinkled up. You would actually look older than you really are. The blackouts, the hangovers, and the loss of key vitamins and minerals, all show up on your skin. When you get rid of alcohol, your skin will have a chance to replenish the lost nutrients, and it will rehydrate itself. Brightness will return to your skin, and your wrinkles will be reduced. Once the toxins have been washed away, your skin will be free from acne, pigmentation, and dryness.

▷ The Risk Of Dementia Lowers

Alcohol does greatly increase your risk of developing dementia. You're probably wondering how this is possible—well, drinking excessively for a long period of time can cause damage to your brain. The weaker your brain is, the higher the risk of developing different kinds of brain diseases. When you give up alcohol, you instantly allow your brain to begin the healing process. As your brain heals itself, it becomes healthier than it was while you were drinking. Researchers carried out an observation at a French hospital between the years 2008 and 2013. They found that 39% of people who were diagnosed with dementia had developed it because of alcohol abuse (Mehmet, 2020). Living with dementia isn't easy. There will come a time when you won't remember your life. All your precious memories will disappear. Giving up alcohol is the best decision you can make for yourself and your family.

▷ Decreases Your Sugar Consumption

It's no secret that alcohol is high in sugar. Those cocktails, licorice shooters, and rum with coke, all have a high amount of sugar in them. Anywhere between seven and ten teaspoons of sugar is present in those drinks, and a cider consists of at least five teaspoons of sugar. Now I know what you're going to say next, that tea and coffee also have high levels of sugar. However, you can manage the amount of sugar you put into your tea and coffee. With alcohol, you don't have a say in how much sugar you are consuming. Drinking excessively can increase your chances of developing diabetes, putting on extra weight, and causing issues in other areas of your body, like rotting teeth. This is all the more reason for you to give up on alcohol; you have a chance to prevent these issues from happening. If you have already developed diabetes or gained weight because of alcohol abuse, you can manage your health better if you stop drinking (Kim et al., 2015).

▷ No IBS or Gastritis

Stomach issues are pretty common among people who consume large amounts of alcohol regularly. You see, the stomach is a sensitive organ. It becomes easily irritated by substances that are highly acidic and strong. The lining of the stomach is affected by alcohol, which causes irritation. Your stomach works overtime to deal with so much alcohol in a short amount of time. This causes acid reflux and indigestion. You could experience symptoms of vomiting, bloating, burning in your chest, and even diarrhea. Studies have shown that alcohol is linked to the bacteria H. pylori, which causes stomach ulcers and gastritis. Giving up alcohol will immediately bring relief to your symptoms, and your stomach will begin to heal itself. Ditch the alcohol, embrace the probiotics and give your gut a chance to heal and work the way it's supposed to.

▷ **Immune System Boost**

Viruses, bacteria, and diseases are common in our world today. Even if you are the most health-conscious person, you could still catch a bug and get sick. For an alcoholic, picking up these viruses and bacteria is relatively easy. Their body will not be able to fight off these illnesses because their immune system is compromised. High levels of alcohol consumption do affect your health, which also places your immune system at risk. Your body needs white blood cells to fight off viruses and bacteria. The more alcohol you consume, the weaker your white blood cells become. This is the body's defense system that fights off illness. When you stop drinking, your body has a chance to produce more white blood cells, and these cells become stronger over time. This will boost your immune system, which will help you fight off bacteria and viruses.

▷ Chances of Reducing Breast Cancer

For women, breast cancer is one of the most feared illnesses to develop. Alcohol contributes to the chances of you developing breast cancer, especially when you drink excessively. According to cancer research conducted in the UK, around 4,400 breast cancer cases were caused by alcohol (Mehmet, 2020), meaning that women who drank a lot had developed breast cancer due to alcohol. Breast cancer is part of the seven other cancers that alcohol is responsible for causing: liver cancer, bowel cancer, mouth cancer, and three types of cancers that affect the throat. This is terrifying. Every drink you have increases your chances of developing any of these cancers. Many people think that it will never happen to them. Understand that your chances of developing cancer are higher than those of people who don't drink.

SELF-ASSESSMENT TOOL

Below is a self-assessment tool to help you assess your relationship with alcohol. The answers that you get will

help you take the necessary steps to recovery. Therefore, it is essential that you take a closer look at your
drinking and find out if there are any problems that
you might not have noticed before.

Question 1

How often do you consume alcoholic beverages?

A. Never
B. Once a month
C. Several times a month
D. Several times a week
E. Daily

Question 2

During the time when you are drinking, how many
drinks do you have per night or day?

A. One or two
B. Three or four
C. Five or six
D. Seven or eight
E. More than 10

Question 3

How often do you have more than six drinks per occasion?

A. Not very often
B. Once every two months
C. Monthly
D. Several times a week
E. Daily

Question 4

During the past year, how often have you noticed that you can't control your drinking?

A. Never
B. A few occasions
C. A few times a month
D. Weekly
E. Daily

Question 5

How often have you noticed that you were unable to do daily tasks because of drinking?

A. Never
B. Sometimes
C. A few times a month
D. Weekly
E. Daily

Question 6

How often have you noticed that you had to have a morning drink to help get you going after a night of excessive drinking?

A. Never
B. A few times a year
C. A few times a month
D. Every week
E. Daily

Question 7

How often do you feel guilty after drinking?

    A. Never, I don't drink much
    B. Sometimes
    C. A few times a month
    D. Weekly
    E. Daily

Question 8

How often have you blacked out after drinking, in the past year?

    A. Never
    B. Sometimes
    C. A few times a month
    D. Every week
    E. Every day

Question 9

How often do you recall injuring someone or hurting yourself after drinking?

    A. I never hurt anyone else or myself when I am drinking
    B. Sometimes
    C. A few times a month
    D. A few times a week
    E. Daily

Question 10

Have any of your family members, friends, or a doctor advised you to cut down on your alcohol consumption because they were worried about your health and safety?

    A. No, I don't drink much
    B. Sometimes my family will mention it
    C. Most of the time
    D. Every day

Results

Mostly A and B

Your drinking is classed as moderate drinking, and it doesn't pose a risk to your health and safety or to those around you. You are a casual drinker who has maintained control of your alcohol consumption. There are limits, and you understand yours very well. You do not have a drinking problem; however, if you feel like you might have issues with drinking alcohol, then you should speak to your doctor about it.

Mostly C

If you have scored mostly Cs, that indicates your drinking problems have just begun. Your alcohol consumption is above moderate, and it's probably already causing problems in your life. You can cut down on your drinking at this stage to prevent falling into addiction. This is the 'in-between' stage where people don't realize that they are developing a drinking problem that could spiral out of control fast. Slow down your drinking and take charge of your life before it gets out of control.

Mostly D and E

If you have scored mostly D and E, then you have a problem with alcohol. This score indicates that you have an unhealthy relationship with alcohol that will ruin your life. Your drinking is hurting you and the people you love. Full-blown alcoholism has taken over your life, and you cannot function without it. This is dangerous for your health and the health of those around you. You have to seek professional help from an alcohol support group or a doctor who can guide you on your next step to becoming sober. It is essential that you stop drinking at this point.

In Closing

This chapter has helped you understand the reasons that played a part in your unhealthy relationship with alcohol. You would have also gained significant insight into where you currently stand with alcohol addiction. I understand that it must have been very challenging for you to examine yourself and figure out why you drink; however, it needed to be done. It's the only way to help you see the seriousness of your drinking. Now that you are aware of how bad things are, you can take the steps needed to help you recover from addiction. The reasons behind your wanting to quit will motivate you to stay committed to this journey. You have also learned about the incredible health benefits that you will reap once you give up drinking alcohol. There is so much to look forward to in life, and that should be motivation enough to get you on the right track. The self-assessment tool was included to help you understand how alcohol has taken over your life. You can choose to take control of your life.

3

STEP 2: CREATE A PLAN

DEVELOP A PLAN TO HELP YOU QUIT DRINKING

This chapter is aimed at helping you find ways to cut down on your drinking. It's vital that you have a clear mind when trying to focus on creating goals that you can work towards during the recovery process. These goals will keep you motivated and eager to continue on your journey, and even when you meet obstacles, you will be able to overcome them because you are highly motivated.

Working On Your Goals

Deciding to quit alcohol is a huge step that involves a lot of self-confidence and courage to make your recovery a success. Studies show that only 25% of people who decide to give up alcohol successfully do so in the long run (Kinreich et al., 2021). There is a huge chance that you might not be successful in your recovery if you don't have the proper motivation to back you up. It's crucial that you go into this process with true intentions of reaching your goals. Some people fail at the first attempt, but the more attempts that are made, the higher chances of success. I guess the only way a person truly knows if they are ready to give up alcohol is when they find themselves at rock bottom, with nothing left to lose. At that moment, you feel empty, exhausted, and you grieve over all the things you have lost because of drinking.

When you sit back and take a look at your life, you realize that there is so much missing. The relationships you have nurtured for years have been destroyed in a matter of days. The career you have been working on since college is now far from your grasp. Your health has taken a hit, and you don't feel like yourself anymore. At this moment, you will decide to change your life for the better or let alcohol destroy you completely. In this chapter, I will help you make your goals a reality. There are certain things that need to be done to ensure that you are taking the right steps towards developing your goals. Below, I have highlighted important tips that will help you work on your goals.

CREATING SMART GOALS

▷ **Step 1: Identify Exactly What You Want**

This step is crucial because this is where you determine what goals you want to set out for yourself. Maybe one of your goals is to quit alcohol. While this is a great goal to work towards, you have to be realistic about it as well. You cannot wake up one day and just stop drinking. There are a lot of things you have to take into consideration first, like your health and the way your body would react to an immediate cut-off from alcohol. So what do you do about this? You could break down your main goal into smaller goals. Using the SMART method, you could create goals that are easier to achieve. SMART goals can be defined as follows:

S- Specific

Be specific about what you want to achieve. Have a good understanding of what needs to be done so that you can achieve your goals.

M- Measurable

Figure out how you are going to measure your progress. This is important for you to see where you are going wrong, or how well you are progressing in your journey.

A- Achievable and Action-Oriented

You should create an action plan that will help you work smarter and faster towards your goals. What will you do to achieve your goals? Do you have a plan that makes your goals achievable?

R- Realistic

Your goals should be realistic. Setting goals that you are not invested in makes them unrealistic. The more you think about what you want, the more realistic your goals should be.

T- Time-based

Set out a reasonable time frame for you to achieve your goals. Keep in mind that you will face obstacles along the way, so ensure that you include time for that as well. Being aware of a timeline will help you stay focused on your plan of action.

Example of a SMART goal plan for cutting down on alcohol

Specific	I will cut down on my alcohol consumption by one drink per day for the next week. Thereafter, I will cut down my drinking by two drinks per day. I will continue this until I reach my goal of drinking only one drink a day.
Measurable	I will record my progress in my journal, or on my desk calendar, every day. I will make a note of the good days and the bad days, so that I can identify what is hindering my progress.
Action	I will buy herbal teas and fresh juices, which I can drink throughout the day. I will only drink alcohol after I have eaten food, and never on an empty stomach. I will also read motivational books on giving up alcohol.
Realistic	I will evaluate my goals daily, to make sure that I can achieve them. If there is anything that feels unrealistic, I will adjust my plan to make sure that my goals are attainable.
Timeline	I will check in with my doctor or my support team every week, and try to stick to my time frame in regard to reducing my alcohol consumption every week.

▷ Step 2: Put Your Plan in Motion

Now is the time to put your plan into action. Think about the week ahead. Do you have anything planned where alcohol is going to be present? Like a day out with your friends or attending a wedding or birthday party. These events often have alcohol available, which could hinder your progress. Planning ahead for these types of situations will give you a heads up as to what to expect. You can work on a plan that will keep you steady on your progress. Ask yourself if it's really important that you attend any of these events. If you have to attend these events, it would be a good idea to set a limit for yourself. Try to stick to a limit of no more than four drinks. Speak to your friends and family about your goals, and ask them to help you stick to your limit.

It won't be easy, and it's best that you understand this before putting yourself in these situations. That is why you should determine how important these events are for you to attend. You should avoid events where alcohol is going to be present, just until you are at a good place with your recovery. Everyday trials and problems that come up because of family, work, friends, relationships, and so on cause stress and frustration, which can often push you towards drinking. Working on a plan of action for these situations is crucial as well. The more you remind yourself that it is a process, and that progress will be made every day, the sooner you will achieve your goals.

Once you have created an action plan to meet your goals, you have to put that plan into action. Go out shopping and get some healthy snacks and juices to help you control your alcohol cravings. Since you are only cutting down your alcohol consumption by one or two drinks per day, consider drinking only after lunch or supper. Draw up a meal plan for the week and tick off each day that you follow through with it. Include the meal times and what you will be eating for each day, and don't forget to include the time that you will start drinking and the limit that you have set for yourself. Reward yourself for each day you stick to your limit. Treat yourself to a slab of your favorite chocolate or a piece of your favorite cake. Don't reward yourself with another glass of alcohol; this would set your progress back a lot. You must understand that you are a real person with real emotions and struggles.

▷ Step 3: Write Down Your Goals and Record Your Progress

Keeping track of your progress is extremely important. Most people who set out to achieve their goals often forget to evaluate their growth, and this causes them to backslide significantly. This is because they don't understand how far they have come or how much work is left to be done. They just find themselves lost in a weak moment, with nothing to reflect on, and this makes them feel like they aren't making any progress, which is how they end up falling back into addiction. There are a number of ways you can track your growth and evaluate any setbacks.

Keep a Recovery Journal

Writing down in a journal is one of the best ways to clear your mind and get things off your chest. You can keep a journal to record your progress and write down all the challenging moments you have faced in that week. Be completely honest and write down your deepest fears and regrets. Don't hold back anything, because the next time you read your journal, you should be able to have a deeper understanding of your feelings throughout this whole process. This will help you see things from a different perspective.

Download a Recovery App

There are several applications available nowadays to help you keep track of your journey through recovery. These apps provide you with daily motivational snippets, and they allow you to customize the tracking tool according to your preference. You could use a checklist or a calendar to keep track of your daily goals. You can also access extra tools, such as member chats, that will help you connect with other women who are on a journey to recovery as well. You can also speak to professionals who can give you advice and work with you. There might be a small fee involved, but it is one of the best ways to keep track of your journey. You can have access to professionals 24/7, from the comfort of your own home.

Create a Checklist

Checklists are a much easier way to track your progress, since they only require you to outline your main objectives for the week or the month. A daily checklist would enable you to set out smaller goals to help you achieve the bigger goals. As you accomplish each task, you can check it off your list. If you were not able to complete any of the tasks you set out for yourself, you simply mark it with an x. You can deal with the setbacks when you have time to reflect on what happened that day. Checklists have worked for many people, and they can be paired with other types of tracking methods.

Create a Vlog

There are thousands of people who use vlogging as a way to share their experiences with the world. This unique way of tracking your growth enables you to share your journey with others who are going through the same things. Making video diaries of your journey, on a weekly or daily basis, can help you make the experience more real. Knowing that there are people out there who look up to you and gain motivation from your videos will keep you motivated to stay committed to the journey. Your followers also become a source of comfort and support, and they can even help you get through the difficult times.

▷ Step 4: Share Your Goals With Others

Sharing your journey with family and friends is a great idea. They can help you achieve your goals by offering support and guidance. Sometimes, family can be our biggest motivation when trying to achieve our goals. However, there are people out there who don't have family around to help them. This doesn't mean that they are alone. Sharing your goals with colleagues, other recovery members, doctors, and therapists is also helpful and motivating. As long as you have some sort of support system, and someone there to celebrate the small milestones with, that is enough to keep you going. Don't feel pressured to talk about your journey with people you don't feel comfortable around. It's your decision with whom you share your journey with, and you shouldn't feel forced or coerced into doing anything.

Goals You Can Work Towards

Here, I'll help you get an idea of the type of goals you can work towards. Of course, your goals will be personal and tailored to your own journey through recovery. However, you can take inspiration from the information that I share with you. Let's get started.

▷ Drinking in Moderation

For adults, drinking in moderation is recommended by the U.S. Department of Health. This means that men should have no more than two drinks per day, and women should stick to having one drink or less per day. The less you drink, the better it is for your health. Heavy drinking, for men, consists of having more than four drinks per day, and more than 14 drinks a week. For women, it consists of having more than three drinks a day, and more than 13 drinks a week. Closely evaluate the amount of alcohol you drink per day and per week, and make a note of this in your journal. It's important to understand how many drinks you are having so that you can work on cutting down the right way. Setting goals is important, as it will help you cut down on your drinking. Your goals should focus on the following:

- Reduce how often you choose to drink
- Cut down on the number of drinks you have per occasion
- Set out a period of time when you will not drink alcohol, thereafter returning to having as few drinks as possible
- Stop all alcohol consumption completely

You can create goals that are similar to this, as long as they are tailored according to your own needs. Remember to be kind to yourself throughout this process. It isn't an easy journey, and you are making a big decision for the betterment of your future. Allow yourself time to get through each goal. Don't be too hard on yourself if you fail; you can always get right back up and try again.

▷ Be Aware of Your Triggers

As a recovering alcoholic, it's imperative that you remain aware of situations that trigger you. This is key to staying committed on your journey to recovery. When you have a good understanding of your triggers, you can plan ahead to avoid them or to manage them when they do occur. Below, I have highlighted the most common triggers:

- being overwhelmed by your emotions
- feeling lonely, hungry, or angry
- mental illness
- physical illness
- stress
- financial problems
- social situations or being around certain friends
- relationship problems
- domestic violence

- sexual abuse

This is a list of the most common triggers; however, each person is different and has their own reasons why they drink. You can make a list of your personal triggers, which will help you gain insight into when and why these situations occur. Planning to avoid or manage these triggers is an important part of the process and should be done immediately.

▷ If-Then Plans

If-then plans were developed to help resolve obstacles that came up during the goal achieving process. The main benefit of the plan is to help you combat temptation and form good habits, which makes it easier to achieve your goals. When you are setting out plans to achieve your goals, you have to also think about where and when you will carry out these plans, and what you will do if met with a certain unforeseen situation. This is a good plan to utilize in your recovery journey, as it will help you prepare for those situations where alcohol will be present. Here are a few examples to help you understand how the if-then plans work.

- If I have to attend a work event, and my colleagues offer me a drink, then I will tell them that I am having no more than two drinks for that day.
- During the week, if I become highly stressed because of kids, then I would rather go for a walk to calm myself down, rather than instantly reach for a drink.
- If I go over my limit for the day, then I will try harder the next day. I will not give up on my recovery.

This is the perfect way to help you stay above these situations. You can have complete control over what happens in your life by planning your responses or reactions to people and situations. The goal-setting process should make more sense to you now. In this chapter, I have explained each process to you step by step. You don't have to make the process seem difficult; all you have to do is:

- Set SMART goals for yourself
- Identify and work on your triggers
- Create if-then plans to help you overcome temptation

In Closing

Goals are the key to making a change in your life. Without goals, you would have no direction in life. Goals give you purpose, and they keep you motivated to achieve success. Your recovery heavily depends on what goals you set out for yourself. Understanding the main reasons why you want to quit alcohol is crucial to the goal-setting process. Set goals that are realistic; there shouldn't be so many that you wouldn't be able to work on them. Create a time frame for to achieve these goals and develop plans to help you achieve them. Then, identify your triggers and make note of them in your schedule or in your diary so that you don't forget. Being aware of your triggers enables you to be one step ahead of them. Next, create if-then plans to help you prepare for situations that will push you towards alcohol. This is a foolproof plan that will help you stay afloat throughout your journey. Most people don't know how to work smart, and that is why they fail. You have the opportunity to work smart and be wise about your goals, so don't miss this opportunity.

4

STEP 3: PLAN AND PREPARE FOR DETOX

PREPARING YOUR MIND AND BODY FOR DETOX

In this chapter, we will focus on preparing you for the detoxing process. I will help you understand what detox really is, and I will show you ways that you can go about it healthily that don't expose you to unnecessary risks. No one quite understands what they're getting into when they sign up for the detox process, and most of the time, people give up because it becomes too much for them to handle. This is because they weren't really prepared for it when they began this journey.

Understanding Detox

I can remember the first time I went through detox. It's an experience you will never forget because of the intense side effects that you have to suffer through. These are the kinds of experiences that stay with you forever. This is good because it reminds you of how hard it is to give up alcohol, and that will prevent you from backsliding on your journey. One of the first things I felt was the intense cravings for alcohol. It felt extreme, and I had a hard time controlling it. Next came the horrible headaches. I can confidently say that they were the worst headaches I have ever experienced in my life. The body chills and the sweats began not too long after the headaches. It just felt like one thing after another was happening to me, and I couldn't even gain control over the first side effect before the rest came along.

I'm not sharing my experience with you to scare you. I want you to understand what I went through, the raw, unfiltered experience that so many people have when giving up alcohol for the first, second, or third time. As incredibly difficult as these withdrawal symptoms were, it was worth it in the end. The energy, freedom, and peace you have when you conquer your addiction makes every withdrawal experience worth it. As a person who went through this, I wholeheartedly encourage you to take that step and battle through the detox. It is worth it, and I want you to experience the same happiness I am feeling now. There is only positivity from here on out.

Causes of Alcohol Withdrawal

Over a certain period of time, your brain and body get used to having alcohol around. So when you decide to quit drinking, your entire body has to rewire itself to function without alcohol in your system. Symptoms of withdrawal can start as early as six to seven hours after your last drink. Anxiety will set in, followed by rapid heartbeat, body chills, and vomiting. The habit of excessive and constant drinking has to be undone, and this isn't an easy process for you or your body. Alcohol withdrawal occurs due to the awakened state that your brain has to be in constantly because of being exposed to alcohol all the time.

So, your brain works harder to try to stay awake so that your nerves can work properly. When you stop drinking, your brain remains in this awakened state. It has become accustomed to being in this state because of prolonged alcohol consumption. This is when withdrawal symptoms start. Even though you are no longer under the influence of alcohol, your body will fight hard to keep you awake. This brings on a lot of different symptoms, such as nausea, hallucinations, headaches, and anxiety.

Who Is at Risk For Alcohol Withdrawal Syndrome?

People who drink excessively on a regular basis are at risk of withdrawal, especially those who have an addiction to alcohol. Even though alcohol withdrawal is most common among adults, in certain instances, it can also happen in teenagers who drink excessively and babies who were exposed to alcohol in the womb. Basically, anyone who has been exposed to alcohol for a prolonged period on a daily basis is at risk of experiencing alcohol withdrawal when they stop drinking. Casual drinkers, who consume less than 10 drinks a week, are not at risk of developing withdrawal. As long as your alcohol consumption is within the guidelines of the U.S. Health Department of Health, you don't have to worry about experiencing withdrawal.

Is This Something You Should Be Concerned About?

Detoxing yourself from alcohol is a difficult process to undergo; some people are worried about the withdrawal symptoms that come with detoxification. These symptoms can range from mild to severe and life-threatening. It is advisable to consult your doctor and seek medical help before starting alcohol detox. You have to give your 100% commitment to this process; come hell or high water, your focus should be there to ensure that your recovery goals are achieved. Understand why it is so important to go through the detoxing phase. Below, we will discuss the importance of alcohol detoxing and how it starts and progresses through the different stages.

▷ **The Importance of Alcohol Detox**

The main reason why this process is so essential is that your body will be flushing out every bit of alcohol from your system during detoxification. You cannot skip this step, or delay it for later. It is the initial step of the recovery process, and you have to be ready before you throw yourself into it. When the withdrawal phase is complete, your journey will become much more bearable from there on out. Just as when you develop a sickness that your body keeps fighting every day, and you notice that before you get better, you actually get a lot worse first. This is when your body is working hard to eliminate all the bad cells. That's when you feel extremely sick and weak. After that phase is over, you recover and bounce back to your old self again. The same thing happens when your body is getting rid of the alcohol that is in your system. You feel a lot worse before you recover completely.

▷ **Symptoms of Alcohol Detox**

Mild symptoms can occur during the process of alcohol detox. Such as:

- Nausea
- Sweating
- Anxiety
- Headaches
- Insomnia

Severe to life-threatening symptoms are as follows:

- Seizures
- Hallucinations
- Tremors
- Disorientation
- Delirium tremens

▷ **Timeline of Alcohol Detox**

Here is an example of a timeline that depicts the process of alcohol detoxing. It starts from an hourly basis and continues over a weekly basis.

- **The First 6 to 12 Hours**

During these initial stages, withdrawal symptoms can vary from mild to moderate. You will experience headaches, body shakes, nausea and anxiety. Your body is beginning to realize that there has been a decrease of alcohol in your system, so it reacts in ways that tell you another drink is needed.

- **The Next 24 Hours**

After 24 hours, more symptoms appear, on top of the other symptoms you have been experiencing already. Your hands begin to shake, you become more disoriented, and seizures might even develop. This is when things start to get real, and it can be a bit scary to go through.

- **The Next 48 Hours**

During this time, symptoms will worsen and become more intense. Vomiting, severe headaches, hallucinations and chills. Most people give up at this stage because it becomes too hard for them to handle. That's why it's important you have a good understanding of what to expect during the different stages of detox.

- **Day Three to Seven**

Your body has been working tirelessly to rid your system of alcohol. By the time you reach the end of day seven, most of your symptoms would come and go. This is the stage where you are at risk for experiencing delirium tremens, a life-threatening symptom that can cause death in certain people.

- **One Week Later**

Your symptoms will begin to wear off at this stage. Medication can be taken to help you manage certain symptoms, and you will feel much better. Although, you are still at risk of experiencing post-acute withdrawal syndrome (PAWS). Anxiety, fatigue, sleep problems, and brain fog are some symptoms of PAWS.

Detoxing Safely at Home

Some people opt for at-home detox during their detoxification process. It is advisable to see your doctor before making the decision to detox at home due to health risks such as experiencing severe withdrawal symptoms. If you suffer with mild or moderate alcohol use disorder, it is possible to safely detox at home, with precautions, proper guidance and support. Having a family member or a friend stay with you during the detoxing process is advisable. If you have an alcohol dependency, it could be dangerous for you to give up drinking suddenly. You have to cut down on your alcohol consumption during the weeks leading up to detox. This will help you detox safely, without shocking your body suddenly. If you begin to experience hallucinations and seizures, you should call the emergency number. Make sure that you have all the important emergency details on hand. Here are some tips to help you detox safely from home. If followed through properly, you can successfully detox at home.

▷ **Keep a Diary to Record and Track Your Alcohol Consumption**

Prior to reducing your alcohol consumption, try to figure out how many drinks you have each day. It's important that you have a number before you start, so that you can measure your progress as you go along. Introduce diary use for one week before you cut down on your alcohol consumption. This will help give you a better understanding of where you are right now. Start by recording how many drinks you have each day, what time of day you prefer to drink, and how many units of alcohol were in each drink you had. Set a goal for yourself, and write down how much alcohol you will be cutting down over the next week or so. Then record your progress as you gradually reduce the amount of alcohol you drink.

▷ Reduce Your Alcohol Consumption by 10% Per Day

Once you have established a stable drinking pattern over one week, you can then try to reduce the amount of alcohol you drink each day by 10%. For instance, if you drink around 15 units of alcohol a day, you can cut that number down to 13 units per day. After a few days, reduce that 13 units by another 10%. Carry on cutting down your alcohol consumption gradually each week. If you develop withdrawal symptoms at any stage, then it could indicate that you have been reducing your alcohol consumption too fast. Take it back a notch, until your body is ready to get back into the process. It won't be easy, and you won't experience the same effect as you did before, but stay committed to the process, it will get better.

▷ **Great Tips to Help You Quit Drinking**

- Eat foods that are low in sugar. Drink lots of water to keep yourself hydrated. You should eat foods that are high in vitamin B, because you have to increase your thiamine levels during this time.
- Remove and throw away all alcoholic drinks from your house.
- Consider switching to a less alcoholic beverage, for example, if you previously drank beers with a high alcohol content, try switching to lighter beers.
- Try having a glass of water in between every drink you have, or consider using alcohol as a mixer.
- You can ask a friend or a family member to keep an eye on how much alcohol you are consuming each day. They could pour out your drinks and record the amount of alcohol you have consumed.
- Avoid caffeinated drinks like coffee and energy drinks, as these cause problems with your sleep.
- Take a vitamin B supplement, preferably one that is 100 mg in strength. It will help get your blood healthy again.

▷ **Create a CheckList for Detox**

Rehab centers usually have their set checklist for patients. If you are detoxing at home, create a checklist of all the important things you have to do. This checklist will help prepare you for detoxing or rehabilitation, by listing all the essential things you have to do to make it a success.

- Call and see your doctor
- Call your mom or any other family member to come to stay with you
- For hydration, buy a lot of water and other non-alcoholic drinks for the house
- Fill your pantry with healthy, well-balanced diet food
- Create your SMART goal plan
- Create your IF-THEN plan
- Have the emergency numbers on your phone or written and visible on the fridge door
- Have the right mindset—you can do this

WHEN SHOULD YOU CONSIDER REHAB?

Alcohol addiction is incredibly difficult to overcome. Millions of people opt for rehab to help them boot their alcohol addiction. There is no shame in asking for help, so if you feel like home detox isn't for you, then you should consider going to rehab. There are so many benefits that come with choosing rehab to help you overcome addiction. Let's look at a few of these benefits below.

▷ Benefits of Choosing Rehab

One of the main benefits of going to rehab is that you have a safe environment to detox and heal yourself. You will be surrounded by medically experienced professionals who will be there to support you and guide you along your journey. These professionals teach you about alcoholism, and they help you understand addiction better so that you can overcome it. In rehab, you will also have peers who are going through their detox process. You can buddy up with someone and help each other through this challenging time. Sharing experiences, and hearing about other people's stories, will encourage you and motivate you to stay committed to your journey. There are also individual programs that can be customized to suit your needs; you don't have to follow a routine or process that doesn't help you. Another amazing benefit of being in rehab is that you learn coping mechanisms and strategies, which help you combat relapse. Rehab gives you more accountability over your progress. You know that there is a time frame given to you that you have to work with, and that you are paying to be there. So, you have to make it worth your while, and you have to make sure that you give your full commitment to the experience.

▷ **The Four Stages of Rehab**

There are four stages to overcome on your journey to becoming sober. Recovering from alcohol addiction is never an easy task, and most people relapse because they don't have an understanding of the various stages of being in rehab. When you understand the process, it makes it easier for you to stay focused on whatever you have to do. Below, we take a look at the different stages of rehab.

Stage 1: Treatment Initiation Stage

The first stage of treatment is reaching out for help. When you seek medical or professional help, you are actually initiating treatment. Asking for help, trying to figure out what can be done to overcome addiction, is an important part of this step. During this stage, your alcohol history will be recorded. A medical professional will work with you, one-on-one, to come up with a treatment plan. Your feelings of denial, the damage caused by the alcoholism, and your reasons for drinking will all be taken into consideration.

Stage 2: Early Abstinence Stage

Once you have decided to quit alcohol for good, the next part of your treatment comes into play. This involves abstaining from alcohol, not touching it, drinking it, or being around it. This can be a difficult phase in your recovery journey because it involves cravings, withdrawal symptoms and triggers that can cause you to relapse. You will identify the different withdrawal symptoms and triggers that tempt you to give up and have a drink. The coping tools that you learn to manage your triggers and withdrawal will stay with you throughout your journey. There are some tips that can help you during this stage.

- Seek the guidance and support of group therapy, and actively participate in sessions.
- Find new ways to keep yourself occupied, rather than turning to alcohol whenever you are bored or upset about something.
- Identify your triggers and find ways to avoid them or overcome them.
- Use spirituality or religion to help you find purpose and hope in your recovery.

Stage 3: Maintaining Abstinence Stage

Once 90 days have passed from the early abstinence stage, you will then move on to the next stage, where you will have to work on maintaining your abstinence. The main focus of this stage is to ensure that you don't relapse. There are certain warning signs that you have to be aware of that can lead to a relapse. You will learn about these signs during this stage, and there will be tools given to you that will help you overcome a relapse. These tools can be used in other areas of your life as well. The less stressed you are in your life, the better it is for your recovery. These tools will help you:

- Develop healthy relationships with family and friends.
- Learn how to manage your finances and find employment.
- Find ways to manage your anger and stress.
- Learn how to make the best of eating healthy foods and exercising.
- Avoid substituting alcohol with other unhealthy substances.

This stage will begin at three months into your recovery and last up to five years of you being sober. You will go in for follow-up counseling from time to time, as soon as your 90 days are over and you have been sent home.

Stage 4: Advanced Recovery Stage

This last stage begins after you have gone five years without drinking alcohol. The advanced recovery stage is an important stage that should not be overlooked. This is where you use all the coping mechanisms and tools that you have learned from rehab, to help you overcome difficult situations in your everyday life. It's a big deal that you have been sober for five years, so take it all in and reward yourself for coming this far. There are some strategies that you could use, during this stage, to help you build on your sobriety.

- Create both long-term and short-term goals.
- Establish a routine for everyday life that you can settle into.
- Build friendships with people who do not drink alcohol.
- Make yourself a part of activities that do not include alcohol, like soccer clubs or pottery classes.
- Find other ways to fill in gaps that may exist in your life. Volunteer at hospitals, participate in the community, and seek spirituality.

How Much Does it Cost to Overcome Addiction?

The price of overcoming alcohol addiction can be unbelievably expensive, depending on the type of program and care that is needed. This can sometimes make a person think twice about recovering. It's important for people to understand their options before they start their recovery journey. There are places that offer rehabilitation services free of charge for those people who can't afford them. And for those who can, there are rehab centers that offer five-star treatment and service. Below, we take a look at the different types of treatment and their costs.

▷ Detox Treatment

Detox treatment ranges from $1,000 to $1,500 for outpatients. If it is part of an inpatient program, then it will be included in the overall cost of that program. Usually, the price depends heavily on the severity of the addiction, and how much care is needed for the individual. This price does include medical costs and other resources needed for detoxing.

▷ Rehab: Inpatient

Inpatient rehab programs range from $6,000 to $20,000 for a 30-day program. These prices may seem out of this world; however, most well-known rehab centers charge around $20,000 for their comfortable facilities and top of the range rehabilitation program, which most celebrities prefer during their recoveries. The usual rehab centers cost around $6,000, and this price includes treatments, counseling services and support. If you want the 60-90 day program, the cost would range from $12,000 to $60,000.

▷ **Rehab: Outpatient**

For addictions that aren't so severe, outpatient programs are available. These programs are cheaper than inpatient programs and usually cost around $5,000 for a three-month program. These programs are designed for people with mild-to-moderate addiction, and the price will depend on how often the individual visits the center and the duration of their visit. This treatment is advised for people who are not full-blown alcoholics, and it is not recommended for those who have a severe addiction to alcohol.

▷ **How to Pay for Rehab**

Insurance is one of the most popular ways that people pay for rehab. The amount that has to be paid by the user depends on the type of insurance and what the company accepts. The following types of insurance cover alcohol addiction:

- insurance that has been financed by the state
- private insurance
- military insurance
- Medicaid or Medicare

Not everyone can afford to have insurance, and because of this, they decide not to seek out help for their recovery. Most people feel like they can never overcome addiction because they don't have the funds to do so, and this keeps them in that cycle of alcohol abuse. However, the government does offer certain rehab centers free of charge to people who cannot afford it. Low income should never be a reason for you to give up on your sobriety. In this situation, it would be best to seek out centers that cater to low income, or are free of charge. There are also rehab centers that offer financial aid, which would be a better choice because most of the free rehabs have a long waiting list. There are many non-profit organizations who offer programs free of charge to people who cannot afford them. The Salvation Army is one such place.

In Closing

In this chapter, we have given you all the information you need to start your recovery. There should be no hesitation in your mind when it comes to the recovery process, because you are now aware of the costs and the stages that are included in the process. You should also have a good understanding of the withdrawal timeline and the symptoms that show up. All the information given to you should prepare you for your journey. I know that you may be scared and worried about how your body will go through the detox process. You are probably wondering whether it would be too much for you to handle, or whether it would be worth all the pain and discomfort. Getting your life back, and living it the way you're supposed to, is worth every detox and recovery process. Now is the time to make a change, so don't delay.

5

STEP 4: MANAGING SOCIAL EVENTS

OVERCOMING SHAME AND STAYING SOBER AT SOCIAL EVENTS

I can clearly remember what my experience was like the first time I attended an event after becoming sober. My anxiety levels were through the roof, and I remember telling myself that everything would go well. I am no longer the person I was before, and I am confident that I will have a good time. I walked into the party confidently, but when I started talking to others, I noticed that my confidence was gradually decreasing. All they could talk about was how bad my alcohol addiction was, and they hope I stay sober in the long run. All I wanted was a few kind words of encouragement and to be treated like any other person at the party. The embarrassment started building up, and all I could think about was how good I would feel after having a drink. I wouldn't feel embarrassed, or tensed up, if I could just have one drink. I quickly pulled myself out of those thoughts and got myself a glass of non-alcoholic wine, and I decided to focus on the good instead of the bad.

I'm not going to sugarcoat anything; my experience was unbearable. But I managed to fix my focus and do the right thing. The key to me staying committed to my sobriety that evening, was when I decided that I'm not going to let the opinions of others affect the way I felt. I knew what my journey was like, and I knew how hard I worked. The only thing that mattered was what I thought about myself. In this chapter, I am going to help you overcome shame and embarrassment when going out to social events, and I am going to show you how to stay sober, no matter what you experience.

Tips to Help You Stay Sober

It can be a real challenge to stay sober during social events. Especially if you were the life of the party at every event you attended. Walking into an event, sober, might feel a bit awkward to you at first. Previously, you would have had a drink before you attended the event, you would have been drinking during the event, and you would also have a few drinks after the event. Basically, you would have been drinking all the time. Now that you are sober, you could you feel uncomfortable and extremely out of your element. However, I'm sure you had a good idea of what to expect before you even entered through that door. The overwhelming anxiety would have been dancing on your chest days before the event even took place. The mere idea of attending an event where alcohol is going to be served, and where your old buddies will be waiting to talk to you about your recovery, is enough to make you feel uneasy and stressed. In the midst of this tension, it's important that you stay sober and focused on your recovery. Below, I have listed a few tips to help you along the way.

▷ **Stay Away From High-Risk Social Events**

During the initial stages of your recovery, it would be a good idea to steer clear of any events where you know that alcohol is going to be present. These events could pose a high risk to your sobriety, so the farther away you are from those situations, the better it will be for you in the long run. You can turn down invites to parties or events and be forthcoming with the host about your recovery. There is no need to lie; recovery is something that you should be proud of and your family and friends should respect your decisions. Yes, you cannot avoid social events forever; this is only temporary until you are at a comfortable place with your sobriety.

▷ Always Have a Plan

If you are well aware of the event ahead of time, and you have to make an appearance because it is important to your family, or friends, or co-workers, then it's wise to have a plan in place. Work on a plan to help you stay away from alcohol and to help you manage your cravings while you are at the event. It isn't going to be easy seeing others having alcoholic beverages around you, but if you have a plan, then it could make you feel a little more in control of your situation. You could ask one of your friends or family members to bring you non-alcoholic beverages that are delicious and fun to drink. They can also check up on you from time to time. Knowing that you have someone watching you will help you power through your cravings and stay focused on your sobriety.

▷ Don't Be Embarrassed or Scared to Say No

When faced with peer pressure, it's crucial that you have the ability to say no. There will be people who are unaware of your recovery, and they could offer you a beer or a glass of wine as a friendly gesture. That is when you have to stand up for yourself and decline their gesture. It can be difficult to say no to family and friends, and sometimes you might even feel scared to say no because you don't want to disappoint anyone on their special day; however, your sobriety comes first. You don't have to be concerned about what others think or feel when it comes to your sobriety. When you say no, you must be confident and assertive so that they know you are being serious. Don't make it seem like you are saying no only because you HAVE to. Show them that you are saying no because you WANT to.

▷ **Keep Yourself Distracted**

The more time you spend thinking about avoiding alcohol, the more intense your cravings are going to be. You have to keep yourself distracted so that your mind can shift its focus from alcohol. Take a walk to clear your mind, go to the buffet table and get yourself a few snacks to munch on, or play a fun game with friends to help you stay entertained. There are lots of other things to do at a party, if you go looking for the right things, you will find them. Distractions can be your only way of avoiding alcohol at social events.

▷ Make a List of All the Reasons Why You Quit Drinking

There could be a number of valid reasons why you decided to quit alcohol in the first place. Those reasons could help you fight off cravings and overcome temptation wherever you go. Make a list of all the reasons you stopped drinking. Maybe you wanted to become sober again for your kids, or maybe your health was taking a hit because of alcohol abuse, and you had to give it up in order to survive. Whatever your reasons are, write them down and carry them in your pocket or put them into a locket and wear it around your neck. This will serve as a reminder of why you no longer wish to entertain alcohol in your life.

▷ Confide in Someone You Trust

Entrust a few people, such as your family or friends, with being your confidant during your recovery process. If you are feeling overwhelmed at the event, you can call one of those people and talk to them about how you are feeling. They can check in with you as well, from time to time during the event.

Great Excuses to Use Whenever Someone Is Urging You to Drink

Sometimes, just saying no isn't enough for some people. You don't have to explain your entire journey of recovery to every person who offers you a drink, it's just unnecessary. So, to help you out, I have listed a few foolproof excuses that you could use every time someone offers you a drink. Read on below.

- "I am taking a break from drinking. It has been affecting my health for a while."
- "I am the designated driver for tonight, so I cannot drink."
- "I am on a course of antibiotics because I haven't been well lately."
- "I have to wake up early tomorrow. I've got an important meeting."
- "Drinking alcohol will mess up my diet; it is high in calories, after all."
- "My partner and I took a bet on who could go the longest without drinking alcohol. So far, I seem to be winning, and I don't want to mess it up."
- "I'm making healthier choices in life and alcohol just isn't healthy enough for me."
- "I want to enjoy my night without the help of alcohol."

- "I have been suffering from awful migraines lately, so I am avoiding alcohol for a while."

These excuses have been used plenty of times to help people get out of situations that involve alcohol. However, I would like to reiterate that "No" is a complete sentence and you don't owe anyone any reason for your actions.

Preparing for a Party in Advance

As a practice run, you will be required to prepare for a party in advance. Think about an event that you have to attend in the near future, where alcohol will be present. Write down five action steps that will help you stay sober at this event. The main idea behind this exercise is to introduce you to planning ahead of time. Most people don't like planning for the future. They just take each day as it comes. However, when you are a recovering alcoholic, it's vital that you plan ahead for these situations. Remember to ask your friends and family for help as well. Support is an important part of planning.

Think About the Following

1. Ensure that they are realistic and foolproof.
2. Seek the help and guidance of a family member or friend to help you plan.

3. Make sure that you are at a good place in your recovery to attend these types of events.
4. Plan for setbacks and think about any possible reason why you might relapse.
5. Give yourself a time frame to be at the event and don't stay longer than required.
6. Identify which friends, family members or co-workers, who drink heavily, will be present at this party.
7. Carry chewing gum and other mini snacks that you can nibble on whenever you feel a craving coming on, and make sure that you buy them in advance.

In Closing

After reading this chapter, you should have the ability to prepare yourself for social events. Having a plan to help keep you sober is an important part of recovery. Falling into temptation is possible during the early stages of recovery, and the more prepared you are, the better your chances of overcoming it. Apart from trying to stay sober at these events, another important aspect must be taken into consideration. Facing your friends, family and strangers with confidence, even though you are in recovery. There is nothing to be ashamed of, and you should walk around with your head held high. Making the decision to quit alcohol takes a lot of courage, and you should never have to feel embarrassed about your relationship with alcohol. Own your truth and be proud of yourself for making it this far.

6

STEP 5: RECOGNIZE THE HIGHS AND THE LOWS

UNDERSTANDING YOUR GOOD DAYS AND YOUR BAD DAYS

As a recovering alcoholic, I never gave much thought to what my good days and bad days would look like. I woke up every morning hoping that it would be a good day. But then I'd feel the cravings start by 10 a.m. My whole body would ache, and my mood would just switch automatically. In my mind, I felt like this whole recovery wasn't working out for me. I didn't realize that there would be bad days ahead of me. I wanted immediate change without having to go through hell first. I remember thinking, this is the lowest I have ever been in my life. I didn't know where to go from there, but I knew that I couldn't stay down.

After a few days, I would wake up feeling great. No cravings, no body aches, and my mood was optimistic and joyful. Then I began to understand that there will be good days, and there will be bad days, but my focus and dedication should remain certain.

Once I got over that phase, my journey really started bearing fruit. My life started changing for the better. I remember when I finished my studies and obtained my degree. I was so excited because I had achieved a huge milestone that I never thought was possible for me. It was time to celebrate my achievement, but I knew that alcohol was not going to be a part of my celebration. Alcohol had held me back from doing the things I needed to do, and I was not going to let it destroy my life anymore. So, I thought of another fun way to celebrate. I booked a fun day at a water park for my entire family. The weather was amazing, and everyone was looking forward to enjoying themselves in the water that day. I went on every water slide, and I spent all day lazing around in the water. This celebration was a thousand times better than getting drunk and blacking out, and I realized that there is so much more to life than just what's in a bottle.

Tracking Your Progress

Once you have achieved sobriety, your journey doesn't end there. Maintaining that sobriety takes a lot of hard work and dedication. It's imperative that you keep track of your progress because it helps you see how much the work you have put into your sobriety is paying off. You have to make sure that you don't fall into a relapse, and you can do this by monitoring your progress on a daily basis. Apps have been developed to help people monitor and track their recovery. These apps can be downloaded on smartphones, laptops and tablets, and they help you stay committed to your recovery. Technology has the ability to reach millions of people in their homes without much effort. So what better way to keep an eye on yourself than with the help of an app. Here are the benefits of using smart apps to help you monitor your recovery.

Benefits of Using Apps

- **Instant access** - You have instant access to a support system that you can reach out to at any time of the day, no matter where you are. There are triggers all around you, and since you always have your smartphone with you, these apps can offer you access to coping tools that help you fight temptation.

- **Privacy** - Your journey through recovery is a personal one, and most people prefer keeping this private. These apps offer you help without disclosing your personal information. You don't have to upload your picture or give your real name if you are not comfortable with that. You can use these apps anonymously, without worrying about your personal details being shared with the world.
- **Availability** - These apps are available to people around the world. You don't have to have money to sign up, or pay any monthly fees. Most of these apps offer their services free of charge to help people with their recovery.
- **Expert advice** - The people who develop these apps often work with experts who have experience with treating people and helping them overcome addiction. You will receive expert advice, and have access to chats with these professionals.

Features on These Apps that Help With Recovery

- **Connecting with others** - You can make connections with other people who are sober. They can help support you through your journey.

- **Locate a meeting** - The app can help you find group meetings that are held in your area.
- **Journaling** - You can create your own journal entries in these apps.
- **Motivational quotes** - These apps also offer daily devotionals that motivate you and keep you in good spirits.
- **Calculators** - This is one of the great features of the app. It has sobriety calculators that keep track of how many days you have been sober, according to the information you put into it.
- **Coping tools** - Step by step coping tools for every stage of recovery.

Five Most Popular Apps You Can Try

- NA Speakers
- AA Speakers
- Nobu
- Recovery Box
- I Am Sober
- Sober Grid

Rewarding Milestones

Milestones are a massive part of all our lives. They represent how far we've come on our journey called life. Turning 30, landing yourself your dream job, getting your driver's license or getting married. These are a few examples of the kind of milestones we celebrate in life. Many people choose alcohol as a way of celebrating, such as throwing a party or having a drink with friends. However, for a recovering alcoholic, alcohol cannot be a part of the celebrations any longer. This doesn't mean that you shouldn't celebrate your milestones. There are plenty of other ways to reward yourself for your success. Every milestone that you achieve in your recovery journey, should be celebrated and enjoyed by you and your loved ones.

Why Is It Important to Celebrate Recovery Milestones?

There are many reasons why it's important that you celebrate your recovery milestones. Below, I list a few of these reasons, to help you gain a deeper understanding. Remember, your journey is special, irrespective of what people say. Your milestones are something to be proud of and this is why you should celebrate them.

▷ **Achieving an Accomplishment**

Your sobriety is the main accomplishment on your journey to recovery. When you celebrate your accomplishments, you are actively recognizing how far you have come. It makes you grateful for all the lessons you have learned, and it teaches you that good things come to those who are committed.

▷ Improves Your Self-Worth

Struggling with alcohol addiction can leave you feeling terrible about yourself. The negative relationship you share with alcohol can drive you to the lowest point in your life. You might find yourself doing things that you would never do, and this makes you lose respect for yourself. All that can change, when you achieve the milestones on your journey. You will feel better about yourself because of all the good choices and hard work that you put into your recovery. That's why it's important to celebrate and reward yourself for all of your achievements.

▷ Keeps You Motivated

Rewarding yourself for your commitment and perseverance will help keep you motivated to complete your journey. When you take the time to recognize your efforts, you fuel yourself with appreciation for your achievements, and this motivates you to stay sober because you see that there are so many good things to look forward to in life. This motivation is vital to your success.

▷ **Share Your Story With Others**

When you celebrate your milestones, you do so with people that you love. Whether they are friends or family, you can inspire any one of them by sharing your story. We never know what's going on behind closed doors, and we have no idea what people are going through. You can help them take the steps needed to change their lives.

▷ **Look Forward to the Future**

Every milestone that you achieve gives you hope for a brighter future. You can wake up every day looking forward to living life, knowing that your worst days are behind you. Celebrate your success, allow yourself to be hopeful and excited about the future. You only have one life, so make sure that you live it to the fullest.

These Are the Milestones that You Should Celebrate

- 24 hours sober (One day)
- 30 days sober
- 90 days sober
- 6 months sober
- One year sober
- 5 years sober

These are the major milestones that you should celebrate in your recovery; however, you can create your own personalized list of milestones that you wish to acknowledge. You can add smaller milestones in between the bigger ones. One week sober, three weeks sober, two years sober, whatever the case may be. You can customize your list with other milestones as well. For example, "attended my first event being sober and managed to overcome temptation." These are significant milestones that should be recognized.

Awesome Ways to Reward Yourself

There are plenty of ways that you can reward yourself for every milestone that you achieve. Alcohol isn't a reward. You will begin to understand this as you progress further on your journey. I have highlighted a few great ways that you can reward yourself after achieving your milestones.

- Treat yourself to a nice, relaxing day at a spa. Enjoy a massage, get a facial, do whatever you want to do.
- Buy yourself a new pair of shoes. Shopping is a reward in itself. Most women love shopping, and we love shoes as well.
- Get yourself a new haircut, or add some highlights to your hair. A new hairstyle is a big

change for a woman. It makes the change very real.

- Start a savings fund. Put aside some money for every milestone you reach. This can be seen as an investment which will pay off in a larger reward.
- Buy yourself something nice, like a chain, that symbolizes your recovery. It's a good keepsake to remind you how far you have come.
- Go out for lunch and a movie, with one of your friends or with your partner. This is a fun way of rewarding yourself that can be shared with those you love.
- Consider getting a tattoo that symbolizes your journey. This can be a great reward, if you are the type of person who loves tattoos.
- Take the day off and binge-watch your favorite TV series, while eating all the junk foods you love.

How to Combat a Relapse

No one starts their journey into recovery expecting to relapse at some point. Nevertheless, there are people who end up relapsing because of a number of different reasons. This doesn't mean that their journey is over. They can always pick themselves up and continue on the road to recovery. Below, I have expanded on why a relapse occurs and what you can do to overcome it. Let's explore this in more detail.

What Causes a Relapse?

No matter how focused and committed you are on your journey, there is a strong chance that you might relapse. However, that doesn't mean you should let it happen. There are a number of reasons why people relapse. The more you understand, the better your chances of beating it. Here are the main reasons why people relapse.

- They don't take their recovery seriously, and they don't make it a priority in their lives.
- They are not aware of what it takes to stay sober, and they start their recovery without being prepared.
- They don't have a support system behind them to help them stay focused.
- They quit alcohol because of someone else, not because they want to quit for themselves.
- They don't have goals or motivation to help them understand why they want to quit.

What You Can Do, After a Relapse, to Help You Get Back on Track

According to the National Institute on Alcohol Abuse and Alcoholism, approximately 90% of alcoholics will relapse within the first four years of recovery (*4 Things to Do after an Alcohol Relapse to Get Yourself Back on Track*, n.d.). Despite these high chances, a relapse doesn't mean you have to fall into addiction again. There are things you can do to make sure that you get back to your sobriety. Below, I have listed a few things that you can do to overcome a relapse.

▷ Stop Drinking Immediately

The moment you realize that you have relapsed, the best thing you can do is stop drinking. I know that you might feel guilty about messing your sobriety up, and that can make you want to continue drinking. But it is in your best interest to stop yourself from drinking any more. The more you allow yourself to fall back into addiction, the harder it will be to recover the next time. You have the opportunity to control your drinking. It is possible to get back to that place of sobriety, all you have to do is display courage and refuse any alcohol from there on out.

▷ Look for Support

Recovery is no walk in the park. It requires a lot of focus, especially when you are going through withdrawal symptoms and detoxing. Seek help from your family and friends. Someone should be there to help you through the process. Even if you have no family or friends that you can count on, support groups offer a lot of support to those who need it. Be open-minded and don't be embarrassed to ask someone to support you through this tough time in your life. Knowing that someone is there to guide you, and watch your every move, will make you more accountable for your actions.

▷ Take Note of What Triggered You

It's important that you identify what caused you to relapse in the first place. Knowing your triggers is vital so that you can take the necessary steps to combat them. These triggers bring back memories of alcohol, and they take you back to the time when you used to drink heavily. Thinking about these things will invoke feelings of desire inside you. That's when the urge to drink becomes stronger and stronger. The more you think about it, the more intense your cravings will become. Whenever you face a trigger, you must be able to use the coping strategies you have learned to help you overcome these triggers.

▷ **Prepare Yourself to Fight Relapses in the Future**

Now that you are aware of what caused your relapse, you can take better steps forward to ensure that you avoid those triggers in the future. You can work with a counselor or an addiction specialist, who can offer you expert advice and guidance on what you should do to make sure that you don't relapse again. Facing your fears is the main step you must take to avoid a relapse. Create a plan to avoid similar situations from occurring in the future. Remember, even though you might have a plan prepared, it could still be difficult to overcome temptation. You have to prepare your mind and your heart for what's coming. As long as you are authentic and remain true to the promises you made to yourself, you will be able to combat relapse.

In Closing

As a recovering alcoholic, it can be extremely difficult to feel good about yourself, especially after a relapse. However, the most important thing that you should always remember is that you don't have to stay down when you fall. You can rise up and continue, stronger than ever. Just because you relapsed, that doesn't mean you are worthless or a waste of time. You did not fail, you just backtracked a bit. Your life is very precious, and maintaining your sobriety is no walk in the park. The main danger behind a relapse is to keep you stuck in addiction. As long as your true intent is to give up on alcohol, everything else will fall into place. There are plenty of people around who want to help you. You need a strong support system in place. If you have experienced a relapse, you must change your mindset and focus on what you can learn from the situation to be better next time. This lesson stays with you throughout your entire life, and it can be used in different situations.

Please remember to love yourself before anything else. You are responsible for your own personal well-being, so make sure that you are always taking care of your emotional and physical needs. This can help you combat relapse faster than you think. If you continue to neglect yourself, your chances of relapsing increase significantly. Be kind to yourself, and be patient, because you are your biggest supporter. You can achieve success in your life, and you can find your sobriety once again. Go easy on yourself, and make sure that you are rewarded for continuing on your journey to sobriety, even after a relapse. Celebrating your milestones is an essential part of your journey. Allow yourself to be happy and let go of the guilt and regret. You don't need money or alcohol to celebrate your achievements. There are many other ways to acknowledge your success. You must remember that there is nothing to be ashamed of, instead, you should be proud of yourself. That is the only way you will achieve success in the end.

7

STEP 6: USE DISTRACTIONS TO YOUR ADVANTAGE

HOW TO USE DISTRACTIONS TO HELP YOU FIGHT CRAVINGS

Cravings are the most challenging aspect of alcohol recovery that a person has to deal with. Whether you are ready to face them or not, these cravings come. If you're not prepared, they will catch you off guard at any time of the day. Most people give in to their cravings as soon as they start their journey into recovery, simply because they are not prepared to handle them.

Finding distractions to help you deal with these cravings is essential to your success in recovery. However, it's important that you find healthy distractions that won't hurt you. In this chapter, I focus on helping you fight off cravings, and I will teach you distraction techniques that will ensure you withstand temptation at all costs. The only way you can overcome temptation, is to take part in meaningful activities that will take your mind off your addiction.

The Importance of Fighting Cravings

Trust me when I say that everyone who is recovering from alcoholism will face temptation almost every day. I remember back to when my journey to recovery began. My cravings were intense, and they grew each day. I was at my wits' end trying to figure out how to fight off these cravings, but then I came up with a few techniques that helped me overcome them. Successfully fighting off the cravings is the key to recovering well. You can learn how to work smart and create distractions for yourself, instead of waiting for the craving to hit and dealing with it when the time comes. It's better to be prepared than to wait for the inevitable. No one can magically make the cravings disappear, but there are ways that you can manage them so they don't consume the progress that you've been making so far.

▷ **Changes in the Brain**

As we learned earlier, cravings stem from changes in brain chemistry. When an individual consumes alcohol daily, the neurotransmitters in their brain become affected by the alcohol. This can lead to an increased desire to drink more often and to drink a larger quantity each time. When you cut down on your drinking, your brain will realize that it isn't getting enough alcohol anymore. This is when feelings of anxiety and stress kick in. Your brain becomes habituated to alcohol, so when you begin to cut down on your alcohol consumption, it affects your brain as much as it affects your body. There is no way that you can prepare your brain for alcohol recovery; it has to go through the withdrawal process so that it can be rewired to function normally without alcohol. This is a long process, as change cannot occur overnight. The chemical neurotransmitters in your brain have to learn how to send messages again without the aid of alcohol.

Your brain has to find ways to help you adapt to the changes that occur around you and within you. When you expose your brain to alcohol for a prolonged period of time, it has no choice but to find a way to help you process your emotions and make decisions, even while you are intoxicated. Your brain cannot shut down just because you have had too much to drink. It has to make sure that all of your organs are pumping and working so that you can stay alive. Can you imagine how much stress your brain will undergo once you decide to quit alcohol? It's like losing a partner you have been sharing a life with for the past couple of years. It will take some time to get used to.

▷ Habit Formation

Consuming alcohol regularly eventually becomes a habit. Running to alcohol whenever you are stressed from an argument with your partner or exhausted after a long day at work also contributes to habit formation. When you are recovering from alcoholism, and you have a heated argument with your partner, what are you going to do? How will you relax after a long day at work? These are important questions to ask yourself so that you can prepare for these situations beforehand. The feelings of comfort and reward after a drink have to be substituted with something else during recovery. Breaking the habit isn't easy, but when you identify that you have a problem that needs a solution, then you can look for alternative ways to help you deal with stress and frustration. There are many other things you can use to comfort and relax yourself apart from alcohol. Break the routine and develop plans to create new, healthier habits that will help you fight off temptation.

▷ Triggers

Your cravings start the moment you are triggered by something. It could be a certain smell, or a memory of something. These triggers are different for each person going through recovery. The moment you are triggered, a strong desire for alcohol takes over, and this is when a lot of people give in and fall back into addiction. They haven't prepared themselves to cope. There are a number of triggers that awaken cravings in recovering alcoholics. Let's take a look at a few of them below. Can you relate to any that are triggers for you?

- Feeling pressured at work
- Getting into an argument with someone
- Feeling sad or depressed
- Feeling angry or annoyed
- The smell of alcohol
- Watching movies or adverts that display alcohol
- Attending events where alcohol is served

▷ **Things That You Can Try in the Moment**

When a craving strikes, it can be very intense and overwhelming. The duration of a typical craving lasts around four to five minutes. The important factor to remember when you are experiencing a craving is to acknowledge that it is happening. Many people try to ignore their cravings; however, this does more harm than good. When you are aware of what is happening, you can work on ways to control the situation. A craving won't last forever; after a while it will subside. Keep reminding yourself that these cravings are not permanent and that eventually you will get over them. Below, I have listed two ways to help you overcome your cravings.

▷ Distract Yourself

Creating a positive distraction is the best way to help you keep busy and make better use of your time so that you are not sitting around daydreaming about alcohol. When your mind is idle, thoughts about alcohol slowly creep into your head. This is how your cravings start, and if not handled in time, you can end up falling back into addiction. By focusing on other things, you are giving yourself the opportunity to fight against your cravings without experiencing so much inner turmoil.

Create a list of distractions that you can keep with you. This list must be easily accessible so that you can review it at any time. Here are a few examples of the kinds of distractions you can use to combat your cravings.

- Clean up your home
- Cook or bake something delicious
- Listen to great music and dance
- Read spiritual books
- Manifest positive words into the universe
- Exercise
- Make yourself a hot cup of tea

- Paint or draw

As you can see, these distractions aren't difficult activities. These are simple tasks that you can do to divert your attention from the cravings. Take some time to sit down and think about what you can do to focus your attention on something else for a bit. Include tasks that help you relax and make you excited enough to forget about the cravings.

▷ **Seek Comfort in Your Friends**

Reaching out to friends can be an excellent way to deal with a craving when it hits. Friends can be a good source of support and motivation during difficult times, especially if they are also on the road to recovery. Sharing each other's pain and progress can be comforting and inspiring. People who are overcoming addiction often choose a support buddy to help them through their journey. This support buddy is available 24/7, since cravings can come at any time of the day or night. Allow yourself to be vulnerable around your trusted friends. You don't have to constantly act like you've got it all figured out. Ensure that you have more than one support buddy on your call list, just in case one of your friends isn't able to take your call at that time.

DISARM Method

DISARM is an acronym for Destructive Images and Self-Awareness Refusal Method. It's a method created by Joseph Gerstein, MD, one of the founders of a well-known nationwide recovery group called SMART Recovery. This strategy was created to help recovering addicts overcome their addiction by disarming their cravings. Here's how it works.

▷ Name the Urge

Give your cravings a name that you will remember. Try something like "the leech" or "the destroyer," anything that you feel is accurate, but also amusing. When you name the craving, you are acknowledging that it exists as something you experience.

▷ Awareness

Pay attention to how you feel when the cravings first start to occur. These signs are important to identify because they will help you deal with the cravings in the early stages.

▷ Refusal

After you've called out the craving using its name and become aware of your feelings, you'll want to instantly refuse the cravings. Don't consider them for even one second. The sooner you consciously choose not to entertain them, the better it will be for your recovery. For example, you could say, "I see you and feel you rising, you leech. I refuse you, you're nothing but a parasite. You don't have power over me."

▷ **Medication**

There are medications, such as Naltrexone and Vivatrol, that can help with managing alcohol cravings. There is no shame in taking medication to help you fight off these cravings. If you believe that they could help you, consider trying one. Your doctor will probably be happy to do what they can to help you fight alcoholism because they know it will make you happier and healthier in the long-run.

▷ **Meditation**

Meditation is a great way to empower you to control your cravings. Mindfulness and meditation have been used for centuries to help people deal with all kinds of physical and emotional issues. There have been studies conducted on how well mindfulness and meditation work for people who are recovering alcoholics. A study carried out by British researchers found that sitting for 11 minutes a day, practicing mindfulness, helped people significantly reduce their alcohol cravings and their consumption (Mindworks, 2018).

Three Common Elements of All Meditation

There are three elements that are common to all forms of meditation.

- Pay attention to the present. Forget about everything else around you and only focus on you and your body in the moment.
- Allow your body and mind to become relaxed and balanced.
- Embrace an attitude that isn't judgmental or biased towards yourself or towards anyone else.

Types of Meditation for Recovery

Consider learning about these types of meditation to begin to understand which you might be interested in trying. You may be surprised at how helpful and empowering they can be. You may also find that one might be more helpful for you when you're anxious and want to relax (e.g., breathing, mindfulness, or guided) versus when you're feeling sad or depressed (e.g., mantra, moving).

- Breathing meditation
- Mindfulness meditation
- Mantra meditation
- Moving meditation

- Guided meditation

Ways That You Can Distract Yourself

You can fill your life up with exciting new activities to keep you busy. It's important to use your time wisely during recovery because the moment your mind goes idle, you will start to entertain thoughts that revolve around alcohol. Below, I have listed a few examples of things you might do to help you refocus your time and energy.

▷ Join a Class

Consider joining an evening dance class that will keep you entertained and on the move. This is a healthy activity to participate in, and you will never be bored with it. You may also meet some interesting people to connect with. There are other less active classes that you can join too, such as a cooking class or a pottery class. Learning a new skill is a great way to distract yourself from your alcohol cravings. It is also a worthwhile activity, which will benefit you. You may even discover an interest or passion you never knew you had.

▷ Volunteer

Volunteering is another great way to distract yourself from the alcohol cravings. There are many places where you could volunteer: Children's homes, hospitals, a women's shelter, or a rehab facility. Helping out others who are also recovering from alcohol addiction will be great for your own recovery. It will open up your eyes to notice how many people are suffering with addiction in one form or another and remind you that you're not alone in this fight.

▷ Join a Gym

Joining a gym is another great way of distracting yourself from your cravings. Keeping your body fit and healthy will help your mind heal and recover as well. Lifting weights is also a great way to let off some steam. There are several forms of exercise you could do to tire your body out naturally so that you can sleep well.

▷ Spend Time With Your Family

Plan some exciting activities that you can do with your family. On weekends, instead of going out to bars and hanging out with friends who drink, consider planning an overnight for your family at the beach or in the mountains. You can do anything, as long as you are around people you love and who love you. That is a great way to refocus yourself from your cravings. Plus, you will feel better about yourself once you have rebuilt your relationships.

Affirmations to Help Keep You on Track

Affirmations are a vital part of your recovery journey. They help keep you focused on the importance of staying sober. When you are having a difficult day, speaking words of affirmation can help to eliminate negativity and promote positivity. Here are a few benefits of using affirmations on your journey.

Benefits of Affirmations

- Eliminate negative thoughts and feelings
- Increase your productivity and performance
- Keep you focused on your goals and objectives
- Increase your mental and physical health
- Motivate you to stay committed to your recovery

Ten Powerful Affirmations You Can Try

- I can beat addiction and I will beat addiction.
- I am becoming a better version of myself every day.
- My addiction has no power over me; I am set free.
- I am in charge of my own life and I will decide how to live it.
- I deserve to be happy and healthy.

- My mind is renewed and I am a new creation.
- I do not hold on to anything negative from my past.
- I am surrounded by love all the time.
- I have a bright future ahead of me.
- I am filled with positivity and hope.

In Closing

You have all the tools you need to overcome your cravings and beat alcohol addiction. I encourage you to create your own list of 10 distractions that you could make use of to help you get your mind off of the cravings. I understand that you might not want to try new things at this point in your life, but opening yourself to new possibilities is crucial to your recovery. You have to reinvent yourself and find new things that fill your life with excitement and give you purpose.

Finally, be sure to list affirmations that speak directly to who you are and what you want for your life. Keep it with you at all times. Pull out this list when you are feeling overwhelmed by negative emotions. Use the DISARM method to overcome your cravings. Planning is the key to staying on top of your cravings. Do whatever it takes to beat addiction! You can do it.

8

STEP 7: CREATE A VALUABLE NETWORK

LEANING ON YOUR FRIENDS AND FAMILY AND BEING A PART OF SUPPORT GROUPS

Having a strong network of people who love and support you is essential for your recovery. I remember that I relied heavily on the support and encouragement from family and friends. In the beginning, I was embarrassed to ask for help. My relationship with alcohol was not something I was proud of, and I cut off a lot of people in my life who only wanted what was best for me. I'd hurt their feelings and closed them off from my life, and not once had I stopped to think about what they were going through. Now that I was beginning my journey to sobriety, how could I ask them to come back into my life and be there to support me? I felt guilty and ashamed. So I stayed away, until things became extremely difficult for me to handle alone.

Eventually, I had to reach out to a family member and ask if they could come over and stay with me for a few days. Without hesitation, my family member agreed to come over. Ideally, that's what family is for. They don't judge you or hold on to grudges; instead, they are forgiving and loving. Everything changed as soon as I had the support of my family. I felt like I could conquer the world, like I could achieve anything I put my mind to. I started getting better each day, and my self-confidence improved greatly.

Reaching Out to Family and Friends

Family is the backbone of every human being on this plant. The word "family" doesn't only relate to biological parents, siblings or other members of an extended family. It also relates to anyone who plays a vital role in your life, who loves you and wants what's best for you. Your family could be your parents, your friends, your caregivers or guardians, your neighbors, your fellow church members and your co-workers. People who love us, and are there for us in good times and bad times, are considered family.

The Role of Family and Friends in Recovery

This part of recovery can be a very humbling experience. Getting in touch with your loved ones is a huge step towards the right direction. Once you have decided that you are going to give up on alcohol once and for all, you can then contact the people around you. Reach out to your family and friends and let them know that you are quitting alcohol, and seeking out treatment. You can ask them to help you find a good rehab center, or you could ask them to check in on you regularly during the detoxing period. Rebuilding your relationships is vital during the recovery stage of addiction. Apart from family and friends, you can reach out to specialists who can help you on your journey. You should never feel ashamed or unwanted because of your experience with alcohol addiction. There are new ways for you to spend time with your family and friends that don't involve alcohol, so don't let that hold you back from reconnecting with them.

There are a lot of people who commence their journey into recovery without their loved ones by their side. Reality is that people who have a toxic relationship with alcohol, often shut out their family and friends. Their behavior changes and they become a completely different person during the course of their addiction. Families break apart, husbands and wives divorce, children get separated from their parents and long-term friendships end. Alcohol literally takes you away from the people you hold close to your heart. We all have some type of duty towards our family and friends, but when you put alcohol above everyone else, you make that a priority. You forget about the responsibilities you have towards others. This selfish behavior pushes people away from your life. Ultimately, no one is going to stick around and wait for you to apologize for how you have hurt them. It goes without saying that your loved ones want to help you conquer this addiction that has taken over your life. But they are hurt, and they feel unwanted in your life. They don't know whether you want their help or not. It's up to you to reach out and welcome them back into your life. There are things that you can do to help them understand how to help you.

Encourage Your Family to Learn About Alcohol Addiction

The more your family understands about alcohol addiction, the more understanding they will become towards you. It is incredibly difficult for someone else to understand what you're going through, especially when they know nothing about your problem. That's when people judge and make up their own scenarios in their heads. Whatever has happened in the past, let it go now. Speak to your loved ones about opening themselves up to learning more about addiction. You can maybe show them a video, or give them a book about addiction. These resources are a great way of helping others understand. Once they have a complete picture, they will be able to look at you through a different perspective.

Help Them Understand When They Can Be There for You, and When Their Presence Isn't Required

Knowing when to be there for you can be confusing for your family and friends. They cannot read your mind, or do as they please. It's normal for your family to want to be there all the time, just to make sure that you are staying sober and that you aren't going behind their backs and having a drink. Even if you do happen to relapse, your family and friends would be the first people who would want to rescue you from that and get you back on the wagon. They jump at the opportunity to help you and guide you, only because they have so much love for you. However, most people who are recovering from alcoholism prefer to have some alone time as well. They don't want to feel like they are being watched constantly, and they don't want their family members to start taking control of their lives by always telling them what to do and where to go. There will be tough moments when you will need the help of your family, and there will be moments when you feel good

162 | RUBI PAGE

about your recovery. It's important that your family understand when to offer their help, and when to let you be. You have to learn how to stand on your own feet as well.

Recovery is a personal journey, and there are a lot of people who don't wish to share any information with their family members. This has to be respected, and family members should not pry too much about what happened. Whenever their help isn't required, you can ask them to kindly take a few steps back. Tell them that you have everything under control for now, and when you need their help, you will come ask for it. In some cases, family members tend to do everything for their loved one that is recovering. This holds them back from standing on their own feet and beating addiction on their own. It's important to your sobriety that you are able to bring yourself out from addiction. Yes, your loved ones can be there to help guide you and support you, but they can do this without enabling you. Whenever you don't want the help of a loved one, you can tell them that you need to do it on your own.

The Role of Support Groups

You will often hear the term "support system" when people talk about recovering from addiction. Support groups are a part of this support system, aside from family and friends. A support group usually consists of a group of people who encourage each other to stay focused during recovery. Even though recovery is a personal journey that people don't like sharing with others, in a support group everyone shares their story with the intention of motivating those around them. It also helps to talk about your experience in a safe place, where there is no judgment from anyone, because they are also on the same journey as you.

Why Are Support Systems Important for Recovery?

Traveling on your journey through recovery can get lonely sometimes. Your family and friends can only be there to a certain extent, and you wouldn't be able to relate to them much because they are not sharing this journey with you. However, when it comes to support groups, that's where you will truly find the support you need. When things get tough, you can take comfort from the peers in your support group. They understand exactly what you are feeling, so they can be more patient with you. Being a part of a support group allows you to express your good feelings and your bad feelings about your journey so far. Here, you can draw positivity and motivation to continue on your journey. A support group also serves as a reminder that you are not the only one who has been caught up in the dark web of alcoholism. There are others who have made wrong choices as well, but they are now changing their lives for the better.

Different Types of Support Groups Available

There are different types of support groups available. Let's take a look at a few of these groups below.

▷ 12-Step Groups

These groups include members who are all participating in the 12-step program of recovery. They meet to discuss each step prior to starting it, and after completion. Advice is given, guidance is offered, and constructive criticism is handed out to help each member perform better in the future.

▷ SMART Recovery Groups

SMART stands for self-management and recovery training. This support group focuses on helping families recover from the trauma and suffering caused by alcohol addiction. Families can attend together and share their experiences with other families.

▷ Women For Sobriety (WFS)

Women for sobriety is a non-profit organization that is aimed at helping women start a new life after recovering from alcohol addiction. Women are given tools to help them stay sober, and they receive support and guidance from people who care about them.

Nine Best Support Groups Online

- Best for women - Women for sobriety
- Best for locating a community of sober people near you - SoberGrid
- Best for overthinkers - SMART support groups
- Best for spirituality - AA
- Best for sharing experiences - Soberistas
- Best for self-empowerment - LifeRing
- Best alternative to face-to-face meetings - In The Rooms
- Best for Buddhist Practices - Recovery Dharma

Making New Friends From Addiction Recovery

It's vital that you make new friends that share the same experience as you do. Meeting people at support groups is a great way to build new friendships that can help make your journey a bit easier. Friends are important in life. And having friends that are sober is important to your sobriety as well. Sooner or later, if you want to stay sober, you have to cut off friends that have a negative relationship with alcohol. Just because you cut these old friends off, doesn't mean that you can't make new friends. These new friends can help you stay focused, and you can have fun together without drinking alcohol. The sooner you make new friends, the better it will be for your recovery.

Tips for Making New Friends

- Be honest and friendly.
- Attend meetings regularly.
- Choose your friends wisely.
- Join more groups.
- Stay connected with alumni.
- Get involved with church or other spiritual events.
- Network with friends of friends.

In Closing

Family is an important part of our lives. No matter how much you may try to shut them out, eventually you will always find a way back. We all experience hard times in our lives, and during these hard times, the support of family is extremely important. By following the advice I have given you in this chapter, you will be able to open up your heart and your life towards your family. On

ALCOHOL RECOVERY FOR WOMEN | 167

this journey through recovery, you will find support all around you. You will never be alone. There are support groups out there, ever ready to help you. Don't be embarrassed about your negative experiences with alcohol, you won't be judged. Instead, you will be welcomed with open arms, as these support groups understand your struggles and they want you to achieve all the goals you set out for yourself.

LEAVE A QUICK REVIEW!

If you liked the book please leave a quick review. Just scan the QR code below!

Thank You!

A FREE GIFT FOR YOU!

9 Common Mistakes To Avoid In Early Alcohol Recovery

Just scan the QR code below to claim Your free gift!

CONCLUSION

This entire book is aimed at showing you that there is life after addiction. Whatever you have been through, is part of your life's journey. We all make mistakes, and sometimes we sit there, in the mess we have created, and wonder what it would be like if only we made the right choices in our lives. Without even realizing it, we spend so much of our time sitting in our mistakes. Years go by, relationships change, and dreams shatter. One day you wake up and you are completely blown away by how vastly life has changed. At this stage, you're probably at your lowest point in life. Nothing left to give, all out of hope, and exhausted from your battle with alcohol addiction. This is the moment where you know that life has to change. This is where step 1 comes into action. Understanding how badly your life has been impacted by alcohol is essential for your recovery. It's imperative that you identify the signs of alcoholism in yourself because it will help you get a clear picture of how far you have gone. You cannot treat the problem unless you are fully aware of the extent of the damage.

Denial is one of the stages that you will pass along the way. Initially, you would have a hard time accepting the truth. You will see the signs, yet you will overlook them. Nobody wants to admit that they have a drinking problem. We all like to think that we have control over every aspect of our lives, and we can't stand it when people point out our weaknesses. This is part of the reason why we choose to deny that we have a real problem. Sometimes we do this because we are afraid of what people might say, or we choose to ignore our issues because when we face them, we know that we have to make a change. Change can be painful. It takes a lot of courage and strength to overcome addiction, and most people aren't ready for that yet. But sooner or later, you have to accept that you have a problem. And this is where your journey to recovery begins. Hereafter, there are certain things that you have to do to make sure that you are on the right track.

Step 2 is about creating SMART goals for your recovery and is one of the key ways to start your journey to sobriety. These goals will give you a clear understanding of what you want to achieve, and what you have to do to get there. Your goals must be specific and clearly defined. They have to be measurable, so that you can evaluate your progress from time to time. Ensure that your goals are realistic and reasonable. Setting goals that are unrealistic could do more harm than good. And lastly, make sure that you have a time frame set out for accomplishing each goal. If you give yourself too much time, you could risk neglecting your goals, and if you give yourself less time, you wouldn't be able to achieve your goals. The timing has to be well planned, and any delays or unforeseen circumstances should be accounted for as well. Planning is key to overcoming hurdles. Whether we admit it or not, the truth is that having a plan always works out to your advantage.

Step 3 reminds you that there are many resources available for people who have been battling alcohol addiction. If you have health insurance, there are rehab centers available that offer you a pleasant and comfortable recovery at their facilities. This often comes with a high price tag, which is normally covered by your insurance. However, if you do not have health insurance, there's no reason to despair. There are many non-profit organizations, such as The Salvation Army, who offer rehabilitation programs free of charge. As long as you are serious about quitting alcohol, there are ways and means for you to be successful. The support you will receive from these rehab centers is amazing. The support of your family and friends is important as well. They can help you during your recovery process, by being there to take care of you during a detox, and guiding you in your sobriety. There are also amazing support groups available, and recovery tracking applications, to help you connect with others who are recovering from addiction as well.

Step 4 involves you working hard to stay sober through your recovery. This takes a lot of planning. You have to evaluate every social event you are invited to, to determine if alcohol will be served. Then, you have to work on a plan to stay sober during these events. I have provided you with excellent tips to help you deal with these situations in step 4. Use them to your advantage, and share them with your friends and family members who are also recovering from alcohol abuse. Step 5 is about celebrating your milestones, another important part of your journey, and it is the most fun part of all! As I have also mentioned in Step 5, it's crucial that you celebrate and recognize your achievements. Celebrating the small wins, as well as the big ones, will keep you motivated to continue on your journey of recovery. Acknowledging the hard work you put into your recovery is important as well. There are ways that you can celebrate without the aid of alcohol.

I'm sure that there are many things that make you happy. You don't need to have hundreds of dollars to celebrate your achievements. In Step 5, I highlighted a few great ideas that you could make use of when celebrating your recovery milestones. Once you have learned how to be thankful for where you are, you will be able to look at yourself differently. Step 6 is all about how to use distractions to fight off cravings. Engaging in meaningful activities to help overcome temptation to drink. There are different distracting techniques such as meditation, mindfulness, Affirmations, going to the gym, coloring, spending time with family, joining a class, anything that will take your mind off the cravings.

Step 7 focuses on helping you rebuild relationships with family and friends who can help you stay sober. Healing broken relationships, and asking for help, is one of the most important aspects of your recovery. Learning to love yourself, and appreciating all the hard work you are putting in, is essential to your growth in recovery. Remember, you are not a robot. You are a human being, with feelings and emotions. You also make mistakes, and there are things you have done which you are not proud of. So be kind to yourself and be patient. Sobriety is waiting for you, all you have to do is trust the process and get back up whenever you fall down. You will face obstacles, and there will be times when you feel discouraged. But don't give up. Stay strong and keep your head held high. You are not your mistakes. Get ready for a new chapter of life that is coming your way!

REFERENCES

Cost of Rehab - Paying for Addiction Treatment. (2018). Addiction Center. https://www.addictioncenter.com/ rehab-questions/cost-of-drug-and-alcohol-treatment/

Excessive Alcohol Use and Risks to Women's Health. (2020, October 23). CDC. https://www.cdc.gov/alcohol/fact-sheets/womens-health.htm

Manning, M. (n.d.). 4 Things To Do After An Alcohol Relapse To Get Yourself Back On Track. *WebMD.* https://www.webmd.com/connect-to-care/addiction-treatment-recovery/alcohol/things-to-do-after-alco hol-relapse

Hanson, J. W., Streissguth, A. P., & Smith, D. W. (1978).

The effects of moderate alcohol consumption during pregnancy on fetal growth and morphogenesis. *The Journal of Pediatrics, 92*(3), 457–460. https://doi.org/10. 1016/s0022-3476(78)80449-1

Jean's Alcoholic Story: I Tried to Blame Everyone and Everything. (2020, September 14). verywell Mind. https:// www.verywellmind.com/jeans-alcoholics-anonymous-story-63503

Kim, J. Y., Lee, D. Y., Lee, Y. J., Park, K. J., Kim, K. H., Kim, J. W., & Kim, W.H. (2015). Chronic alcohol consumption potentiates the development of diabetes through pancreatic β-cell dysfunction. *World Journal of Biological Chemistry, 6*(1), 1–15. https://doi.org/10. 4331/wjbc.v6.i1.1

Kinreich, S., McCutcheon, V. V., Aliev, F., Meyers, J. L., Kamarajan, C., Pandey, A. K., Chorlian, D. B., Zhang, J., Kuang, W., Pandey, G., Viteri, S. S.-S. de., Francis, M. W., Chan, G., Bourdon, J. L., Dick, D. M., Anokhin, A. P., Bauer, L., Hesselbrock, V., Schuckit, M. A., & Nurnberger, J. I. (2021). Predicting alcohol use disorder remission: a longitudinal multimodal multi-featured machine learning approach. *Translational Psychiatry, 11*(1). https://doi.org/10.1038/s41398-021-01281-2

Lam, A. H. (2021, May 12). 15 Foolproof Excuses for Not Drinking Alcohol. *Tosaylib*. https://tosaylib.com/ foolproof-excuses-not-to-drink-alcohol/

Alcohol Use Disorder - Symptoms and Causes.. (2018, July 11). Mayo Clinic. https://www.mayoclinic.org/ diseases-conditions/alcohol-use-disorder/symptoms-causes/syc-20369243

Stedman, E. (2021, August 9). Benefits of not drinking alcohol: 16 amazing health benefits of ditching the booze. *GoodtoKnow*. https://www.goodto.com/wellbe ing/effects-of-alcohol-283521

Mende, M. A. (2019). Alcohol in the Aging Brain – The Interplay Between Alcohol Consumption, Cognitive Decline and the Cardiovascular System. *Frontiers in Neuroscience, 13*. https://doi.org/10.3389/fnins.2019. 00713

Mukamal, K. J., Robbins, J. A., Cauley, J. A., Kern, L. M., & Siscovick, D. S. (2007). Alcohol consumption, bone density, and hip fracture among older adults: the cardiovascular health study. *Osteoporosis International, 18*(5), 593–602. https://doi.org/10.1007/s00198-006-0287-7

O'Hara, K. (2017, April 3). 5 Ways to Find Motivation To Quit Drinking Alcohol. *Alcohol Mastery.* https://alco holmastery.com/5-ways-to-find-motivation-to-quit-drinking-alcohol/

A quote by Christine Caine. (n.d.). Goodreads. Retrieved April 6, 2022, from https://www.goodreads.com/ quotes/7072229-sometimes-when-you-re-in-a-dark-place-you-think-you-ve

101 Inspiring Recovery Quotes About Addiction.. (2018, April 27). Landmark Recovery. https://landmarkrecov ery.com/addiction-recovery-quotes/

Roerecke, M., Vafaei, A., Hasan, O. S. M., Chrystoja, B. R., Cruz, M., Lee, R., Neuman, M. G., & Rehm, J. (2019). Alcohol Consumption and Risk of Liver Cirrhosis. *The American Journal of Gastroenterology, 114*(10), 1574–1586. https://doi.org/10.14309/ajg. 0000000000000340

Savin, J. (2020, July 31). 23 proudly sober celebrities who say quitting alcohol changed their lives. *Cosmopolitan.* https://www.cosmopolitan.com/uk/ body/health/a33323277/sober-celebrities/

Scoccianti, C., Lauby-Secretan, B., Bello, P.-Y., Chajes, V., & Romieu, I. (2014). Female Breast Cancer and Alcohol Consumption: A Review of the Literature. *American Journal of Preventive Medicine, 46*(3, Supplement 1), S16–S25. https://doi.org/10.1016/j.amepre.2013.10.031

10 Benefits of Alcohol Treatment. (n.d.). Cirque Lodge. Retrieved April 18, 2022, from https://www.cirquelodge.com/alcohol-rehab/benefits/

Why Do Alcoholics Drink? 4 Reasons Behind Alcohol Abuse. (2020, November 14). Genesis Recovery San Diego. https://www.genesisrecovery.com/why-do-alcoholics-drink/

Why Support Systems Are Important in Recovery | Sea Change Recovery. (2020, April 1). Sea Change Recovery. https://seachangerecovery.com/los-angeles-addict-support-systems/

Alcohol and Meditation. (2018, June 30). Mindworks. https://mindworks.org/blog/meditation-to-stop-drinking/

Avoiding triggers that will lead to an alcohol relapse. (2020, June 17). The Freedom Center. https://www.thefree

domcenter.com/avoiding-triggers-that-will-lead-to-an-alcohol-relapse/

Hester, R. (2021, April 6). 11 tips on how to deal with urges and cravings to drink and use drugs. *CheckUp & Choices.* https://checkupandchoices.com/11-tips-and-ways-to-deal-with-urges-and-cravings-to-drink-and-can-be-helpful-in-dealing-with-urges-to-use-drugs-too/

Hurley, T. (2020, July 12). Six types of meditation for recovery. *English Mountain Recovery.* https://englishmountain.com/six-types-meditation-addiction-recovery/

Sack, D. (2014, April 3). What is healthy distraction?: How distraction can prevent relapse. *Psychology Today.* https://www.psychologytoday.com/gb/blog/where-science-meets-the-steps/201404/what-is-healthy-distraction

Urge surfing: Guided meditation script [Worksheet]. (n.d.). Therapist Aid. https://www.therapistaid.com/worksheets/urge-surfing-script.pdf

Printed in Great Britain
by Amazon

13290520R00108